COMPETITIVE
SPIRITS
& Other
Peak Performers

VGM Careers for You Series

CAREERS FOR
COMPETITIVE
SPIRITS
& Other
Peak Performers

Jan Goldberg

VGM Career Horizons
NTC/Contemporary Publishing Group

Library of Congress Cataloging-in-Publication Data

Goldberg, Jan.
    Careers for competitive spirits & other peak performers / Jan Goldberg.
      p. cm. — (Careers for you series)
    ISBN 0-8442-2063-9 (cloth). — ISBN 0-8442-2065-5 (paper)
      1. Vocational guidance. I. Title. II. Title: Careers for competitive
spirits and other peak performers. III. Series.
HF5382.G648   1999
331.7′02—dc21   98–43810
                                           CIP

Published by VGM Career Horizons
A division of NTC/Contemporary Publishing Group, Inc.
4255 West Touhy Avenue, Lincolnwood (Chicago), Illinois 60646-1975 U.S.A.
Copyright © 1999 by NTC/Contemporary Publishing Group, Inc.
Printed in the United States of America
International Standard Book Number: 0-8442-2063-9 (cloth)
                                         0-8442-2065-5 (paper)
99 00 01 02 03 MV 18 17 16 15 14 13 12 11 10 9 8 7 6 5 4 3 2 1

This book is dedicated to my incredible husband, Larry, and my precious daughters, Sherri and Debbie. Thank you for bringing so much joy into my life.

Contents

Acknowledgments

The author gratefully acknowledges the following individuals for their contributions to this project:

- The numerous professionals who graciously agreed to be profiled in this book

- My dear husband, Larry, for his inspiration and vision

- My children, Deborah, Bruce, and Sherri, for their encouragement and love

- Family and close friends—Adrienne, Marty, Mindi, Cary, Michele, Paul, Michele, Alison, Steve, Marci, Steve, Brian, Steven, Jesse, Bertha, Uncle Bernard, and Aunt Helen—for their faith and support

- Diana Catlin for her insights and input

- Betsy Lancefield, editor at VGM, for making all projects rewarding and enjoyable

CHAPTER ONE

Attention: Competitive Spirits

"A horse never runs so fast as when he has other horses to catch up and outpace." OVID

C ompetitive spirits love a challenge. They perform at their best when they have deadlines to meet, quotas to break, competitors to beat. Obstacles are puzzles to be solved, problems to be overcome—not barriers blocking the way. No opposition is too large to tackle. In fact, the higher the stakes, the more difficult the rules, the greater the satisfaction.

Most competitive spirits follow this credo in every facet of their lives—whether it's in the sports arena, vying for points; in educational institutions, competing for the highest grades; or on the job, striving for the best performance. When it comes to planning a professional career, competitive spirits know there is no greater thrill than being able to put their talents to the test while earning a living at the same time.

Competitive spirits approach a career choice with as much enthusiasm and forethought as they would need for any life challenge. True competitors plan ahead and make sure they know all their options. They study the rules and requirements of the game, become familiar with the playing field, and research the competition they'll face.

In the pages ahead you'll learn about a number of careers that might match your desire for a competitive atmosphere. Breaking in and rising to the top won't be a piece of cake for most of these careers. But that's the way competitive spirits like it. They don't want anything handed to them easily; they want to prove themselves and earn their own successes every step of the way.

Do You Have What It Takes?

Before we examine the many options open to you, let's make sure you're a genuine peak performer who will thrive in a competitive atmosphere. Take the following quiz. Answer each question True or False.

1. The closer the deadline, the higher your energy level—and your productivity.

2. "Winner takes all" is your motto. No playing it safe and hedging your bets.

3. You want your paycheck to reflect your actual work output, to increase—or decrease—as a direct result of your efforts.

4. You think quickly on your feet.

5. You firmly believe that those who hesitate come in dead last.

6. You're always the first to know.

7. The words "I can't" are not in your vocabulary.

8. You thrive on pressure. Stress is just another five-letter word.

9. You work hard and play hard. Couch potatoes are the other guys.

10. You believe that no problem is insurmountable and that quitting is not an option.

Being the quick thinker that you are, you know that answering each question with True means you possess the personality, makeup, and qualities needed to do well in a competitive atmosphere. You've chosen this book because it's the right one for you. You're on the right track, a winning track. Read on to see your career options.

Competitive Careers

Competitive spirits do well in any number of competitive careers, but the ability to perform at a peak level isn't the only factor to consider. We all have our own special interests and areas where we excel. What follows is an overview of different careers where your ability to compete will be highly valued. Also included are possible settings in which you could find employment. But each position has its own requirements, working conditions, benefits, and downsides, and those will be discussed in detail in the chapters ahead.

Sales

Whether selling insurance, real estate, antiques, or exotic automobiles, sales professionals (in addition to being knowledgeable about their product) know how to interest customers in their merchandise. They have excellent verbal and written skills. They are good at public speaking and giving convincing demonstrations. They also shine at social interaction, networking, and making contacts.

The income of many salespeople depends on the amount of business they bring in. Some are paid solely on a commission basis, earning a percentage for each product or service they sell. Other situations offer a salary plus commission. Often salespeople are rewarded with bonuses and extra perks, such as the use of a free car and cell phone, for meeting and surpassing the quotas their employers set.

Possible Job Settings

Sales professionals work for many types of concerns and handle a variety of products and services. Retail sales runs the gamut from department stores to specialty shops. You could sell cars or airplanes, washing machines or tractor trailers. Salespeople work in real estate, insurance sales, and the travel industry. Some sales teams work for manufacturers, wholesalers, and distributors, selling food to supermarkets and restaurants or expensive x-ray equipment to hospitals and doctors' offices.

Marketing

Marketing specialists are true strategists. As top executives or as team members, marketers determine the need and demand for products or services, identify potential customers, set appropriate prices to ensure a profit, and work on getting the word out and publicizing their offerings. They work with other related professionals, including sales staff, product developers, public relations experts, advertisers, and promoters.

While developing a new product and watching it succeed can be very thrilling and rewarding, marketers can also risk losing their job if a product doesn't perform as predicted.

Possible Job Settings

Marketing professionals work within departments of large corporations or for small firms. They find their niche in advertising agencies or public relations firms. Employers can be anyone with a product, idea, or service to sell, and they range from educational institutions to the military.

Advertising

Advertising departments in large corporations (or separate advertising firms) usually focus on three main activities: account services, creative services, and media services.

The account services department assesses the need for advertising and maintains the accounts of clients. The creative services department develops the subject matter and the way the advertising will be presented. This department is supervised by a creative director, who oversees the copy chief and art director and their staffs.

The media services department is supervised by the media director, who oversees planning groups that select the particular media in which the advertising will appear—for example, radio, television, newspapers, magazines, or outdoor signs.

All positions within advertising are fast paced, pressured, and extremely competitive. The bottom line is consumer dollars. Advertisers, along with a team of marketers, publicists, and sales staff, must vie with their competitors for every one of those dollars.

Possible Job Settings

Advertising specialists find work in many of the same settings as their marketing colleagues. Nonprofit associations, utility companies, government organizations, consulting firms, and educational facilities are just a few of the many possibilities.

Public Relations

The public relations expert faces challenges every day, dealing mainly with the employer's image and the public's perception of it.

Public relations professionals can also help shape companies and the way they perform. By means of research and evaluation, PR practitioners find out the expectations and concerns of the public and report on their findings.

Public relations is a relatively young field, founded less than a hundred years ago. Back then, PR was defined more as press agentry and publicity. As the profession grew and changed, those aspects became less the work of the PR professional and fell more into the realm of publicists and advertising and marketing professionals.

Today, public relations encompasses a variety of job titles and professional responsibilities. Modern public relations includes the consultant, the corporate communicator, the investor relations specialist, the public information officer, the community liaison, the government mediator, the troubleshooter, the spokesperson, and the media coordinator.

Possible Job Settings

PR professionals work in every sector, from the corporate world to the sporting world, from government departments to health and medical facilities. You'll find public relations specialists wherever there's an image to convey—or correct. Options include virtually every industry—from entertainment to travel, from food to health care.

Labor unions, universities, state-owned corporations, publishing houses, and broadcasting companies all utilize the services of PR staff. And though the settings may vary, the backbone of every PR professional's job description is his or her role as communicator.

Law

Not every lawyer makes headline news, sets precedents for new laws, or gets to handle landmark cases. But even those working quietly, away from media attention, still feel the excitement of the game, the thrill of the chase, the satisfaction of a successful deal closing or the right verdict coming in.

And although not every law specialty provides the challenges that competitive spirits need, several do. This particularly includes criminal and trial law, which are worth considering as possible career choices.

Getting into law school is also a competitive process. Only those with the best GPAs and LSAT scores make it. Once in, the workload for students can be overwhelming. Then there's the bar exam to pass and just the right law firm to land a job with.

On the job, the challenges are there every day—briefs to research and write, arguments to put forward, battles to win or lose. Practicing law can be the perfect career choice for many peak performers.

Possible Job Settings

Lawyers can work for large or small private law firms or as in-house counsel for concerns such as banks, publishing companies, or a myriad of other corporations.

Many legal experts work for the government as public defenders or prosecutors. However, the majority of lawyers work on their own in private practice.

Research

Just as reporters strive to get to the story first and land the big scoops, so do research scientists hope to be the first to discover medical cures or breakthrough technology. Funding is often limited and the pressure is high to produce results.

While images of the serious scientist working alone in a lab at a leisurely pace are often depicted in film and television, the reality is quite different. Funding can dry up, sponsorship withdrawn—and jobs lost—if the research doesn't bear fruit.

In addition to possessing a competitive spirit, research scientists must have extensive training and in-depth knowledge of their field. They often spend years studying, earning master's and doctoral degrees, before landing full-time jobs. Income can be sporadic, based upon grants won and lost.

Possible Job Settings

Research scientists may find work in private or government-funded research labs, in medical schools and other university departments, in hospitals, and for pharmaceutical companies.

Entertainment

The entertainment world is a tough industry because there are plenty of talented people out there and the competition is stiff. Although "overnight success" is a catch phrase often tossed around, the truth is most actors and musicians struggle for many years before even getting a role or having a song released, never mind a starring role or platinum album.

Competitive spirits seeking a career in entertainment have to be thick-skinned as well as talented. Rejection is the name of the game.

Possible Job Settings

In addition to the three most obvious settings—the big screen, television, and stage—entertainers work in a variety of other environments, such as nightclubs or comedy clubs and private affairs such as weddings and bar mitzvahs. They may deliver singing telegrams, work as clowns or magicians at children's birthday parties, or train those who want to find their place in the entertainment industry.

Other Competitive Careers

There are a host of other competitive careers including (but not limited to) writing, reporting, professional sports, and politics.

Getting the Inside Scoop

What better way to learn about a profession than by talking to people who have worked in the field? A few phone calls to the right human resource department or the alumni office of your school can hook you up with someone whose brain you can pick—or even follow around for a day or two.

To better help you make an informed choice, several professionals have been interviewed within these pages. Their firsthand accounts tell you what their work involves, how they got started, and how you can enter the profession.

In addition, at the end of each chapter you will find the names and addresses of professional associations for many of the positions discussed in this book. Many publish newsletters that list job openings. Most provide pamphlets with career information. Some material is free; others might cost a nominal fee of a dollar or two. Make your request via phone call or letter.

CHAPTER TWO

Careers in Sales

"Everyone lives by selling something." ROBERT LOUIS STEVENSON

F or the competitive spirit, sales is often a natural career choice. Within some areas of sales, your paycheck can directly reflect your effort. The harder you work and the more successful you are, the larger the financial reward.

Sales professionals can compete with themselves and watch their checks increase from month to month. They can also compete with colleagues and win bonuses for having the highest sales in any given period.

In addition, the playing field spreads to competitors in similar businesses. Not only do sales professionals have to outdo themselves and other employees, they have to make sure their companies' products or services win out over the competition. Avis Car Rental's famous slogan, "We're #2. We try harder," is a great illustration of that point.

The field of sales encompasses a wide range of job settings, products and services, as well as methods of selling. Sales can be broken into the following three main categories:

Retail

Services

Manufacturing and Wholesale

There are also several sales categories that do not fit snugly into those three and have carved their own niches:

Insurance Sales

Real Estate Sales

Travel Agents

Let's examine each of them.

Retail Sales

Millions of dollars are spent each day on all types of merchandise—everything from sweaters and books to food and furniture. Whether selling clothing, cosmetics, or automobiles, a sales worker's primary job is to interest customers in the merchandise. This may be done by describing the product's features, demonstrating its use, showing various models and colors, and pointing out why products will benefit the customer or client.

For some jobs, particularly those involving the selling of expensive and complex items, special knowledge or skills are needed. For example, workers who sell personal computers must be able to explain to customers the features of various brands and models, the meaning of manufacturers' specifications, and the types of software that are available. In jobs selling standardized articles such as food, hardware, linens, and housewares, sales workers may often do little more than take payments and bag purchases.

Some retail sales workers also receive cash, check, and charge payments; handle returns; and give change and receipts. Depending on the hours they work, they may have to open or close the cash register. This may include counting the money in the cash register; separating charge slips, coupons, and exchange vouchers; and making deposits at the cash office. Sales workers are often held responsible for the contents of their register, and, in many organizations, repeated shortages are cause for dismissal.

In addition, sales workers may help stock shelves or racks, arrange for mailing or delivery of a purchase, mark price tags, take inventory, and prepare displays. Sales workers must be aware of not only the promotions their stores are sponsoring, but also those that are being sponsored by competitors. Also, they often must recognize possible security risks and know how to handle such situations.

Consumers often form their impressions of a store by its sales force. The retail industry is very competitive, and, increasingly, employers are stressing the importance of providing courteous and efficient service. When a customer wants a product that is not on the sales floor, for example, the sales worker may check the stockroom and, if there are none there, place a special order or call another store to locate the item.

Job Settings for Retail Sales Workers

Sales workers are employed by many types of retailers to assist customers in the selection and purchase of merchandise. The largest employers of retail sales workers are department stores. Other types of employers include specialty shops, boutiques, independently owned stores, and large chain outlets, such as those selling hardware or office supplies.

Catalogue and on-line sales are two additional avenues for those interested in sales careers.

Training for Retail Sales Workers

Usually, there are no formal education requirements for this type of work. Employers look for candidates who enjoy working with people and have the tact and patience to deal with difficult customers. Among other desirable characteristics are an interest in sales, a neat appearance, and the ability to communicate clearly and effectively. Before hiring, some employers conduct background checks, especially for jobs involving high-priced items.

In most small stores, an experienced employee or the proprietor instructs newly hired sales personnel in making out sales checks and operating the cash register. In larger stores, training programs are more formal and usually are conducted over several days.

As salespeople gain experience and seniority, they usually move to positions of greater responsibility and are given their choice of departments. This often means moving to areas with potentially higher earnings and commissions. The highest earning potential is usually found selling big-ticket items. This work often requires the most knowledge of the product and the greatest talent for persuasion.

In years past, capable sales workers without a college degree could advance to management positions, but today's large retail businesses generally prefer to hire college graduates as management trainees, making a college education increasingly important. Despite this trend, capable employees without a college degree should still be able to advance to administrative or supervisory work in large stores.

Opportunities for advancement vary in small stores. In some establishments, advancement opportunities are limited because one person, often the owner, does most of the managerial work. In others, however, some sales workers are promoted to assistant managers.

Retail selling experience may be an asset when applying for sales positions with larger retailers or in other industries, such as financial services, wholesale trade, or manufacturing.

Earnings in Retail Sales

The starting salary for many part-time retail sales positions is the federal minimum wage. In some areas where employers are having difficulty attracting and retaining workers, wages are much higher than the established minimum.

The following chart shows average weekly earnings by salespeople in several industries.

Motor vehicle and boats—$479

Radio, television, hi-fi, and appliances—$415

Furniture and home furnishings—$354

Hardware and building supplies—$323

Parts—$319

Apparel—$255

Compensation systems vary by type of establishment and merchandise sold. Some sales workers receive an hourly wage. Others receive a commission or a combination of wages and commissions. Under a commission system, salespeople receive a percentage of the sales they make. These systems offer sales workers the opportunity to significantly increase their earnings, but they may find their earnings depend on their ability to sell their product and the ups and downs in the economy.

In addition, nearly all sales workers are able to buy store merchandise at a discount, often from 10 to 40 percent below regular prices. In some cases, this privilege is extended to the employee's family as well.

Services Sales

Services sales representatives sell a wide variety of services. For example, sales representatives for data processing services firms sell complex services such as inventory control, payroll processing, sales analysis, and financial reporting systems. Hotel sales representatives contact government, business, and social groups to solicit convention and conference business for the hotel.

Fund-raisers plan programs to raise money for charities or other nonprofit causes. Sales representatives for temporary help services firms locate and acquire clients who will hire the firm's employees.

Telephone services sales representatives visit commercial customers to review their telephone systems, analyze their communications needs, and recommend services such as installation of
additional equipment. Other representatives sell automotive leasing, public utility, burial, shipping, protective, and management
consulting services.

Services sales representatives act as industry experts, consultants, and problem solvers when selling their firms' services. The
sales representative, in some cases, creates demand for his or her
firm's services. A prospective client who is asked to consider buying a particular service may never have used, or even been aware
of a need for, that service. For example, wholesalers persuaded to
order a list of credit ratings to check their customers' credit prior
to making sales may discover that the list could be used to solicit
new business.

There are several different categories of services sales jobs.

Outside sales representatives call on clients and prospects at
their homes or offices. They may have an appointment, or they
may practice cold calls, arriving without an appointment.

Inside sales representatives work on their employers' premises,
assisting individuals interested in the company's services.

Telemarketing sales representatives sell exclusively over the
telephone. They make large numbers of calls to prospects,
attempting to sell company services themselves or to arrange
appointments between the prospects and an outside sales representative. Some sales representatives deal exclusively with one, or
a few, major clients.

Despite the diversity of services being sold, the jobs of all services sales representatives have much in common. All sales representatives must fully understand and be able to discuss the
services their companies offer.

Also, the procedures they follow are similar. Many sales representatives develop lists of prospective clients through telephone
and business directories, asking business associates and customers for leads, and calling on new businesses as they cover

their assigned territory. Some services sales representatives acquire clients who inquire about their companies' services.

Regardless of how they first meet the client, all services sales representatives must explain how the services being offered can meet client needs. This often involves demonstrations of company services. Sales reps must answer questions about the nature and cost of the services and try to overcome objections in order to persuade potential customers to purchase the services. If they fail to make a sale on the first visit, they may follow up with more visits, letters, or phone calls. After closing a sale, services sales representatives generally follow up to see that the purchase meets the customer's needs and to determine if additional services can be sold.

Because services sales representatives obtain many of their new accounts through referrals, success hinges on developing a satisfied clientele who will continue to use the services and will recommend them to other potential customers. Like other types of sales jobs, a services sales representative's reputation is crucial to his or her success.

Services sales work varies with the kind of service sold. Selling highly technical services, such as communications systems or computer consulting services, involves complex and lengthy sales negotiations. In addition, sales of such complex services may require extensive after-sale support. In these situations, sales representatives may operate as part of a team of sales representatives and experts from other departments. Sales representatives receive valuable technical assistance from these experts. For example, those who sell data processing services might work with a systems engineer or computer scientist, and those who sell telephone services might receive technical assistance from a communications consultant. Teams enhance customer service and build strong long-term relationships with customers, resulting in increased sales.

Because of the length of time between the initial contact with a customer and the actual sale, representatives who sell complex technical services generally work with several customers simultaneously. Sales representatives must be well organized and efficient in scheduling their time.

Selling less complex services, such as linen supply or exterminating services, generally involves simpler and shorter sales negotiations.

A sales representative's job may likewise vary with the size of the employer. Those working for large companies generally are more specialized and are assigned territorial boundaries, a specific line of services, and their own accounts. In smaller companies, sales representatives may have broader responsibilities: administrative, marketing, or public relations, for example, in addition to their sales duties.

Job Settings for Services Sales Representatives

Services sales representatives hold more than five hundred thousand jobs nationwide. More than half work for firms providing business services, including computer and data processing, advertising, personnel supply, equipment rental and leasing, mailing, reproduction, and stenographic services.

Other sales representatives work for firms that offer a wide range of other services, such as business services (advertising, computer and data processing, personnel supply, mailing), engineering and management, personal, amusement and recreation, automotive repair, membership organizations, hotels, motion pictures, health, and education.

Training for Services Sales Representatives

Many employers require services sales representatives to have a college degree, but requirements may vary depending on the industry a particular company represents. Employers who market advertising services seek individuals with a college degree in advertising or marketing or a master's degree in business administration; companies that market educational services prefer individuals with an advanced degree in marketing or a related field.

Many hotels seek graduates from college hotel administration programs, and companies that sell computer services and telephone systems prefer sales representatives with a background in computer science or engineering. College courses in business, economics, communications, and marketing are helpful in obtaining other jobs as services sales representatives.

Employers may hire experienced, high-performing sales representatives who have only a high school diploma. This is particularly true for those who sell nontechnical services, such as exterminating, laundry, or funeral services.

Many firms conduct intensive training programs for their sales representatives. A sound training program covers the history of the business; origin, development, and uses of the service; effective prospecting methods; presentation of the service; answering customer objections; creating customer demand; closing a sale; writing an order; company policies; and using technical support personnel.

Sales representatives also may attend seminars on a wide range of subjects given by in-house or outside training institutions. These sessions acquaint employees with new services and products, help them maintain and update their sales techniques, and may include motivational or sensitivity training to make sales representatives more effective in dealing with people. Sales staffs generally receive training in the use of computers and communications technology in order to increase their productivity.

In order to be successful, sales representatives should have pleasant, outgoing personalities and good rapport with people. They must be highly motivated, well organized, and efficient. Good grooming and a neat appearance are essential, as are self-confidence, reliability, and the ability to communicate effectively.

Sales representatives should be self-starters who have the ability to work under pressure to meet sales goals.

Sales representatives who have good sales records and leadership ability may advance to supervisory and managerial positions. Frequent contact with business people in other firms provides sales workers with leads about job openings, enhancing advancement opportunities.

Earnings for Services Sales Representatives

The median annual income for full-time advertising sales representatives is about $26,000. Representatives selling other types of business services earn about $30,200. Earnings of representatives who sell technical services generally are higher than earnings of those who sell nontechnical services.

The average yearly income for entry-level sales is about $36,000, ranging up to $63,000 for senior sales staff. Earnings of experienced sales representatives depend on performance. Successful sales representatives who establish a strong customer base can sometimes earn more than their managers. Some sales representatives earn well over $100,000 a year.

Sales representatives work on different types of compensation plans. Some get a straight salary; others are paid solely on a commission basis—a percentage of the dollar value of their sales. Most firms use a combination of salary and commissions.

Some services sales representatives receive a base salary plus incentive pay that adds 50 to 70 percent to the base salary. In addition to the same benefits package received by other employees of the firm, outside sales representatives have expense accounts to cover meals and travel, and some drive a company car. Many employers offer bonuses, including vacation time, trips, and prizes, for sales that exceed company quotas.

In spite of all the perks, with fluctuating economic conditions and consumer and business expectations, earnings may vary widely from year to year.

Manufacturing and Wholesale Sales

Articles of clothing, books, and computers are among the thousands of products bought and sold each day. Manufacturers' and wholesale sales representatives play an important role in this process. While retail sales workers sell products directly to customers, manufacturers' representatives market company products to other manufacturers, wholesale and retail establishments, government agencies, and institutions. Regardless of the kinds of products they sell, the primary duties of these sales representatives are to interest wholesale and retail buyers and purchasing agents in their merchandise and to ensure that any questions or concerns of current clients are addressed. Sales reps also provide advice to clients on how to increase sales.

Depending on where they work, sales representatives have different job titles. Many of those representing manufacturers are referred to as manufacturers' representatives, and those employed by wholesalers generally are called sales representatives. Representatives who sell technical products, for both manufacturers and wholesalers, are usually called industrial sales workers or sales engineers. In addition to those employed directly by firms, manufacturers' agents are self-employed sales workers who contract their services to all types of companies.

Manufacturers' and wholesale sales representatives spend much of their time traveling to and visiting with prospective buyers and current clients. During a sales call, they discuss the customers' needs and suggest how their products or services can meet those needs. They may show samples or catalogs that

describe items their companies stock and inform customers about prices, availability, and how their products can save money and improve productivity. In addition, because of the vast number of manufacturers and wholesalers selling similar products, they try to beat competitors by emphasizing the unique qualities of the products and services offered by their companies. They also take orders and resolve any problems or complaints with the products and services.

These sales representatives have additional duties as well. For example, sales engineers, who are among the most highly trained sales workers, typically sell products that require technical expertise to install and use. Sales engineers may also need to familiarize clients with support products for their purchases, such as material-handling equipment, numerical-control machinery, and computer systems.

In addition to providing information about their firms' products, these workers help prospective and current buyers with technical problems. For example, sales engineers may recommend improved materials and machinery for a firm's manufacturing process, draw up plans of proposed machinery layouts, estimate cost savings from the use of their equipment, and negotiate the sale—a process that may take several months.

Sales engineers must also provide follow-up services, keeping close contact with clients to ensure they renew their contracts. Sales engineers may work with engineers in their own companies, adapting products to special customer needs.

Increasingly, sales representatives who lack technical expertise work as a team with a technical expert. For example, sales representatives make the preliminary contacts with customers, introduce the products, and close the sales. However, technically trained representatives will attend the sales presentations to explain and answer technical questions and concerns. In this way, the sales representative is able to spend more time maintaining and soliciting accounts and less time acquiring technical knowledge.

Obtaining new accounts is an important part of the job. Sales representatives follow leads from other clients, from advertisements in trade journals, and from participation in trade shows and conferences. At times, they make unannounced visits to potential clients. In addition, they may spend a lot of time meeting with and entertaining prospective clients during evenings and weekends.

Sales representatives also analyze sales statistics, prepare reports, and handle administrative duties, such as filing their expense account reports, scheduling appointments, and making travel plans. They study literature about new and existing products and monitor the sales, prices, and products of their competitors. Supervisors track the daily activities of sales reps—where they have been, who they have seen, and what they have sold.

In addition to all these duties, manufacturers' agents must manage their businesses. This requires organizational skills as well as knowledge of accounting, marketing, and administration.

Some manufacturers' and wholesale sales representatives have large territories and do considerable traveling. Because a sales region may cover several states, they may be away from home for several days or weeks at a time. Others work near their home bases and do most of their traveling by automobile. Because of the nature of the work and the amount of travel, sales representatives typically work more than forty hours per week.

Sales Managers

Sales managers direct their firms' sales programs. They assign sales territories and goals and establish training programs for their sales representatives. Managers advise their sales representatives on ways to improve their sales performance. In large, multiproduct firms, they oversee regional and local sales managers and their staffs. Sales managers maintain contact with dealers and distributors. They analyze sales statistics gathered by their staffs to determine sales potential and inventory requirements and monitor the preferences of customers. Such information is vital to develop products and maximize profits.

Sales managers also have to go out in the field to see their sales reps. The reps can't afford to take the time to come to the office and lose sales. They also make sure the reps are using the right techniques in order to maximize sales.

Training for Manufacturers' and Wholesale Sales Representatives

The background needed for sales jobs varies by product line and market. As the number of college graduates has increased and the job requirements have become more technical and analytical, most firms have placed a greater emphasis on a strong educational background. Nevertheless, many employers still hire individuals with previous sales experience who do not have a college degree. In fact, for some consumer products, sales ability, personality, and familiarity with brands are more important than a degree.

On the other hand, firms selling industrial products often require degrees in science or engineering in addition to some sales experience. In general, companies are looking for the best and brightest individuals who have the personal characteristics and desire necessary to sell.

Many companies have formal training programs for beginning sales representatives that last up to two years. However, most businesses are accelerating these programs to reduce costs and to expedite the return from training. In some programs, trainees rotate among jobs in plants and offices to learn all phases of production, installation, and distribution of the products. In others, trainees may take formal classroom instruction at the plant, followed by on-the-job training under the supervision of a field sales manager.

In some firms, new workers are trained by accompanying more experienced workers on their sales calls. As these workers gain familiarity with the firm's products and clients, they are given increasing responsibility until they are eventually assigned their own territories. As businesses experience greater competition, increased pressure is placed upon sales representatives to produce faster.

These workers must stay abreast of new merchandise and the changing needs of their customers. Sales representatives should enjoy traveling because much of their time is spent visiting current and prospective clients. They may attend trade shows where new products are displayed or conferences and conventions where they meet with other sales representatives and clients to discuss new product developments. In addition, many companies sponsor meetings for the entire sales force to discuss sales performance, product development, and profitability.

Earnings for Manufacturers' and Wholesale Sales Representatives

Compensation methods vary significantly by the type of firm and the products sold. However, most employers use a combination of salary and commission or salary plus bonus. Commissions are usually based on the amount of sales, whereas bonuses may depend on individual performance, on the performance of all sales workers in the group or district, or on the company's performance.

Median annual earnings of full-time manufacturers' and wholesale sales representatives is about $36,000, although some might start as low as $16,000 and range up to $62,000 or more. Earnings vary by experience and the type of goods or services sold.

In addition to their earnings, sales representatives are usually reimbursed for expenses, including transportation costs, meals, hotels, and entertaining customers. They often receive benefits such as health and life insurance, a pension plan, vacation and sick leave, personal use of a company car, and frequent flyer mileage. Some companies offer additional incentives, such as free vacation trips or gifts for outstanding sales workers.

Unlike sales reps working directly for a manufacturer or wholesaler, manufacturers' agents work strictly on commission. Depending on the types of products they are selling, their levels of experience in the field, and the number of clients they have, their earnings can be significantly higher or lower than for those working in direct sales. In addition, because manufacturers' agents are self-employed, they must pay their own travel and entertainment expenses as well as provide for their own benefits, which can be significant costs. Frequently, promotion takes the form of an assignment to a larger account or territory where commissions are likely to be greater.

Experienced sales representatives may move into jobs training new employees on selling techniques and company policies and procedures. Those who have good sales records and leadership abilities may advance to sales supervisors or district managers. Others find opportunities in buying, purchasing, advertising, or marketing research. For many sales reps, the end goal is to climb the ladder in sales and transfer into marketing.

Insurance Sales

Insurance agents and brokers sell individuals and businesses insurance policies that provide protection against loss. Policies cover health, life, automobiles, jewelry, personal valuables, furniture, household items, businesses, real estate, and other properties.

Agents and brokers prepare reports, maintain records, and, in the event of a loss, help policyholders settle insurance claims. Specialists in group policies may help employers allow employees to buy insurance through payroll deductions. Insurance agents may work for one insurance company or as independent agents selling for several companies. Insurance brokers do not sell for a particular company but place insurance policies for their clients with the companies that offer the best rates and coverage.

Life insurance agents and brokers are sometimes called life underwriters. Property/casualty insurance agents and brokers sell policies that protect individuals and businesses from financial loss as a result of automobile accidents, fire or theft, or other property losses. Property/casualty insurance can also cover workers' compensation, product liability, or medical malpractice. Many life and property/casualty insurance agents also sell health insurance policies covering the costs of hospital and medical care or loss of income due to illness or injury.

Because insurance sales agents obtain many new accounts through referrals, it is important that agents maintain regular contact with their clients to ensure their financial needs are being met as personal and business needs change. Developing a satisfied clientele who will recommend an agent's services to other potential customers is a key to success in this field.

Training for Insurance Salespeople

For jobs selling insurance, companies prefer college graduates, particularly those who have majored in business or economics. Some hire high school graduates with potential or proven sales ability or who have been successful in other types of work. In fact, most entrants to agent and broker jobs transfer from other occupations, so they tend to be older, on average, than entrants to many other occupations.

Many colleges and universities offer courses in insurance, and some schools offer a bachelor's degree in insurance. College courses in finance, mathematics, accounting, economics, business law, government, and business administration enable insurance agents or brokers to understand how social, marketing, and economic conditions relate to the insurance industry.

It is important for insurance agents and brokers to keep current with issues concerning clients. Changes in tax laws, government benefit programs, and other state and federal regulations can affect the insurance needs of clients and how agents conduct business. Courses in psychology, sociology, and public speaking can prove useful in improving sales techniques. In addition, some basic familiarity with computers is very important. The use of computers to provide instantaneous information on a wide variety of financial products has greatly improved agents' and brokers' efficiency and enabled them to devote more time to clients.

All insurance agents and brokers must obtain a license in the states where they plan to sell insurance. In most states, licenses are issued only to applicants who complete specified courses and then pass written examinations covering insurance fundamentals and the state insurance laws.

New agents usually receive training at the agencies where they work and, frequently, also at the insurance company's home office. Beginners sometimes attend company-sponsored classes to prepare for examinations. Others study on their own and accompany experienced agents when they call on prospective clients.

Insurance agents and brokers need to be enthusiastic, outgoing, self-confident, disciplined, hard working, and able to communicate effectively. They should be able to inspire customer confidence. Some companies give personality tests to prospective employees because personality attributes are so important in sales work. Since agents and brokers usually work without supervision, they must be able to plan their schedules well and have the initiative to locate new clients.

An insurance agent who shows sales ability and leadership may become a sales manager in a local office. A few advance to agency superintendent or executive positions. However, many who have built up a good clientele prefer to remain in sales work. Some, particularly in the property/casualty field, establish their own independent agencies or brokerage firms.

Earnings for Insurance Salespeople

The median annual earnings of salaried insurance sales workers is about $31,000, but workers can start as low as in the teens and range up to $75,000 or more.

Most independent agents are paid on a commission-only basis. Sales workers employed by an agency may be paid in one of three ways—salary only, salary plus commission, or salary plus bonus. Commissions, however, are the most common form of compensation, especially for experienced agents. The amount of the commission depends on the kind and amount of insurance sold and whether the transaction is a new policy or a renewal. Bonuses are usually awarded when agents meet their production goals or when an agency's profit goals are met.

Many agencies also pay for automobile and transportation expenses, conventions and meetings, promotion and marketing expenses, and retirement plans. All agents are legally responsible for any mistakes they make, and independent agents must purchase their own insurance to cover damages from their errors and omissions.

Real Estate Sales

Buying or selling a home or an investment property is not only one of the most important financial events in peoples' lives, but one of the most complex transactions as well. As a result, people generally seek the help of real estate agents or brokers.

Real estate agents and brokers need to have a thorough knowledge of the housing market in their communities. They must know which neighborhoods will best fit their clients' needs and budgets. They have to be familiar with local zoning and tax laws and know where to obtain financing. Agents and brokers also negotiate price between buyers and sellers.

Brokers

Brokers are independent businesspeople who, for a fee, sell real estate owned by others. They also rent and manage properties. In closing sales, brokers often provide buyers with information on loans to finance their purchases. They also arrange for title searches and for meetings between buyers and sellers when details of the transactions are agreed upon and the new owners take possession. A broker's knowledge, resourcefulness, and creativity in arranging financing that is most favorable to the prospective buyer often mean the difference between success and failure in closing a sale.

In some cases, agents assume the responsibilities in closing sales, but in many areas this is done by lawyers, lenders, or title companies. Brokers also manage their own offices, supervise associate agents, advertise properties, and handle other business matters.

Agents

Real estate agents generally are independent sales workers who provide their services to licensed brokers on a contract basis. In return, the broker pays the agent a portion of the commission earned from property sold through the firm by the agent. Today, relatively few agents receive salaries from brokers or realty firms. Instead, most derive their incomes solely from commissions.

Real Estate Sales Responsibilities

When you work with customers in real estate, the most important thing is to learn how to listen to their needs. Clients will describe their dream home, telling you everything they want, but often it's more than they can afford. You have to go through that list and pick out their priorities. Is it necessary for them to have four bedrooms, for example, or will three do? Do they want one story or two? Do they need a room to serve as an office?

At that point, the agent or broker calls in a mortgage broker, and they go through the buyers' qualifications and see where they sit financially. It's very important to prequalify buyers. Agents can then see if the buyers can afford a $100,000 house, for example, or something more or less costly.

Then the agent goes to the computer and pulls up everything that's in that price range, picking out the most viable possibilities and starting from the top. It's a progression that involves a lot of elimination.

Then, the house hunting begins. Agents spend a lot of time showing homes to prospective buyers. Once a home has been found and the contract has been signed by both parties, the real estate broker or agent must ensure that all special terms of the contract are met before the closing date. For example, if the seller has agreed to a home inspection or termite and radon inspections, the agent must make sure that they are done. Also, if the seller has agreed to any repairs, the broker or agent must see to it that they have been made, otherwise the sale cannot be completed.

Increasingly, brokers and agents must handle environmental problems or make sure the properties they are selling meet environmental regulations. For example, they may be responsible for dealing with problems such as lead paint on the walls. While many other details are handled by loan officers, attorneys, or other people, the agent must check to make sure that they are completed.

Because brokers and agents must have properties to sell, they spend a significant amount of time obtaining listings (owner agreements to place properties for sale with the firm). They spend much time on the telephone exploring leads gathered from various sources, including personal contacts. When listing properties for sale, agents and brokers make comparisons with similar properties that have been sold recently to determine fair market value.

Most real estate agents and brokers sell residential property. A few, usually those from large firms or specialized small firms, sell commercial, industrial, agricultural, or other types of real estate. Each specialty requires knowledge of that particular kind of property and clientele.

Although real estate agents and brokers generally work in offices, much of their time is spent showing properties to customers, analyzing properties for sale, meeting with prospective clients, researching the state of the market, inspecting properties for appraisal, and performing a wide range of other duties. Brokers provide office space, but agents generally furnish their own automobiles.

Training for Real Estate Agents and Brokers

All states including the District of Columbia require real estate agents and brokers to be licensed. This means that every prospective agent must be a high school graduate, be at least eighteen years old, and pass a written test. The examination, which is more comprehensive for brokers than for agents, includes questions on basic real estate transactions and on laws affecting the sale of property.

Most states require candidates for the general sales license to complete at least thirty hours of classroom instruction and those seeking the broker's license to complete ninety hours of formal training in addition to experience in selling real estate (generally one to three years). Some states waive the experience requirements for the broker's license for applicants who have bachelor's degrees in real estate. A small but increasing number of states require that agents have sixty hours of college credit—roughly the equivalent of an associate's degree.

State licenses generally must be renewed every year or two, usually without reexamination. Many states, however, require continuing education for license renewal.

Personality traits are as important as formal credentials. Brokers look for applicants with pleasant personalities and neat appearances. Honesty, maturity, tact, and enthusiasm for the job are required in order to motivate prospective customers in this keenly competitive field. Agents also should be well organized and detail oriented as well as have good memories for names and faces, and for business details such as taxes, zoning regulations, and local land-use laws.

The beginner usually learns the practical aspects of the job under the direction of an experienced agent. This includes focusing on the use of computers to locate or list available properties or identify sources of financing.

Many firms offer formal training programs for both beginners and experienced agents. Larger firms generally offer more extensive programs than smaller firms. More than one thousand universities, colleges, and junior colleges offer courses in real estate. At some, a student can earn an associate's or bachelor's degree with a major in real estate; several offer advanced degrees.

Many local real estate boards that are members of the National Association of Realtors sponsor courses covering the fundamentals and legal aspects of the field. Advanced courses in appraisal, mortgage financing, property development and management, and other subjects also are available through various National Association of Realtors affiliates.

Earnings for Real Estate Agents and Brokers

Commissions on sales are the main source of earnings for real estate agents and brokers. Few receive a salary. The rate of commission varies according to the kind of property and its value. The percentage paid on the sale of farm and commercial properties or unimproved land usually is higher than that paid for selling a home.

Commissions may be divided among several agents and brokers. The broker and the agent in the firm that obtained the listing generally share their part of the commission when the property is sold; the broker and the agent in the firm that made the sale also generally share their part of the commission.

Although an agent's share varies greatly from one firm to another, often it is about 50 or 60 percent of the total amount received by the firm. The agent who both lists and sells the property maximizes his or her commission.

Real estate agents and brokers who work full-time have median yearly earnings of about $31,500. But earnings could be as low as $10,000 or less or run up to $75,000 or more.

A beginner's earnings often are irregular because a few weeks or even months may go by without a sale. Although some brokers allow an agent a drawing account against future earnings, this practice is not usual with new employees. The beginner, therefore, should have enough money to live on for about six months or until commissions increase.

The Downsides

In addition to lean income periods, sometimes a deal can fall through at the last minute. For example, buyers might get prequalified for a mortgage, based on their income and amount of debt, if any, and other factors. But another financial examination is conducted just before closing. If the buyers have purchased new furniture, for example, or in some other way changed their financial picture, it can kill the deal.

Agents also have to be very careful when dealing with new clients who are strangers. This is especially true for women realtors. Brokers will encourage their agents to work in pairs if possible and to always arrange the first meeting with the client to take place at the office, not at the property. Another precaution is not to take clients in your car, but have them follow in their own cars.

There are always times when you show a client twenty properties and don't sell a thing. You can spend a lot of time, but most agents don't look at it as wasted time. It gives you a chance to increase your knowledge of different properties new to the market. You can always use that information for the next call.

Travel

Out of all the industries worldwide, the travel and tourism industry continues to grow at an astounding rate. In fact, according to the Travel Works for America Council, it is the second largest employer in the United States (the first being health services). Nearly everyone tries to take at least one vacation every year, and many people travel frequently on business. Some travel for education or for that special honeymoon or anniversary trip.

Constantly changing air fares and schedules, a proliferation of vacation packages, and business/pleasure trip combinations make travel planning frustrating and time consuming. Many travelers, therefore, turn to travel agents, who can make the best possible travel arrangements for them.

Depending on the needs of the client, travel agents give advice on destinations; make arrangements for transportation, hotel accommodations, car rentals, tours, and recreation; or plan the right vacation package or business/pleasure trip combination.

They may also provide information on weather conditions, restaurants, tourist attractions, and recreation. For international travel, agents also provide information on customs regulations, required papers (passports, visas, and certificates of vaccination), and currency exchange rates.

Travel agents must learn about all the different destinations, modes of transportation, hotels, resorts, and cruises, then work to match their customers' needs with the services travel providers offer.

Travel agents generally work in an office and deal with customers in person or over the phone. But first of all, they listen to the needs of their customers, then try to develop the best package for each person. They may work with a variety of clients, from affluent, sophisticated travelers to students trying to save money and travel on a budget. They could book a simple, round-trip air ticket for a person traveling alone or handle arrangements for hundreds of people traveling to a convention or conference.

Some travel agents are generalists; they handle any or all situations. Others specialize in a particular area such as cruise ships or corporate travel. Travel agents gather information from different sources. They use computer databases, attend trade shows, and read trade magazines. They also visit resorts or locations to get firsthand knowledge about a destination.

They have to keep up with rapidly changing fares and rates, and they have to know who offers the best packages and services. Their most important concern is the satisfaction of their clients.

Since travel providers understand that travel agents are more likely to sell what they have enjoyed, most travel agents are offered free trips to help familiarize them with a particular cruise line, safari adventure, exclusive resort, or ecological tour. Travel agents also receive discounted travel on other business trips, as well as on their own vacations.

Travel agents often base recommendations on their own travel experiences or those of colleagues or clients. Travel agents may visit hotels, resorts, and restaurants to judge, firsthand, their comfort, cleanliness, and quality of food and service.

The Downsides

The downside, however, according to many travel agents, is that they seldom have enough free time to do all the traveling they would like. They are often tied to their desks, especially during peak travel periods such as the summer or important busy holidays. A newcomer would get to take at least one week a year, more once they've gained some seniority.

The work can also be frustrating at times. Customers might not always know what they want, or their plans can change, and, as a result, the travel agent might have to cancel or reroute destinations that had already been set. There are times when things go wrong. There could be a snowstorm at an airport and missed connections, or someone in the family becomes ill and a client has to cancel a cruise reservation at the last minute.

Training for Travel Agents

Formal or specialized training is becoming increasingly important for travel agents since few agencies are willing to train people on the job. Many vocational schools offer three- to twelve-week full-time programs, as well as evening and Saturday programs. Travel courses are also offered in public adult education programs and in community and four-year colleges. A few colleges offer bachelor's and master's degrees in travel and tourism. Although few college courses relate directly to the travel industry, a college education is sometimes desired by employers. Courses in computer science, geography, foreign languages, and history are most useful. Courses in accounting and business management also are important, especially for those who expect to manage or start their own travel agencies. Several home-study courses provide a basic understanding of the travel industry.

The American Society of Travel Agents (ASTA) and the Institute of Certified Travel Agents offer a travel correspondence course. Travel agencies also provide on-the-job training for their employees, which focuses on computer instruction. These computer skills are required by employers to operate airline reservation systems.

Experienced travel agents can take an advanced course (leading to the designation of Certified Travel Counselor) offered by the Institute of Certified Travel Agents. The institute awards certificates to those completing an eighteen-month part-time course. It also offers certification, called Designation of

Competence, in North American, Western European, Caribbean, or South Pacific tours.

Travel experience is an asset since personal knowledge about a city or foreign country often helps to influence clients' travel plans. Experience as an airline reservation agent also is a good background for a travel agent. Travel agents need good selling skills. They must be pleasant and patient and able to gain the confidence of clients.

Beginners often start working side by side with someone more experienced in the agency. They might be placed in a specific department handling, for example, European travel, cruises, or car rental and air fares. Much of their time will be spent coordinating and arranging details.

Travel agents must also compete with all the other travel agents in the field and need to know how to promote their services. This may be accomplished by presenting slides or movies to social and special interest groups, arranging advertising displays, and suggesting company-sponsored trips to business managers.

Those who start their own agencies generally have experience in established agencies. They must generally gain formal supplier or corporation approval before they can receive commissions. Suppliers or corporations are organizations of airlines, ship lines, or rail lines. The Airlines Reporting Corporation, for example, is the approving body for airlines. To gain approval, an agency must be in operation, be financially sound, and employ at least one experienced manager/travel agent.

Earnings for Travel Agents
Salaries vary according to the region in which you work and your experience. Depending on the agency, you could start out on an hourly wage or a yearly salary. Some travel agents prefer to work on a commission basis. That way, the more trips they sell, the more money they earn. A salary plus commission provides the best compensation combination.

Travel agents who are good salespeople can also earn bonuses or more free or discounted trips. If your pay is initially low, it can be offset by this added benefit.

Experience, sales ability, and the size and location of the agency determine the salary of a travel agent. According to a Louis Harris survey, conducted for *Travel Weekly Magazine*, annual earnings for travel agents are as follows:

less than one year experience—$16,400

from one to three years—$20,400

from three to five years—$22,300

from five to ten years—$26,300

more than ten years—$32,600

Salaried agents usually have standard benefits, such as insurance coverage and paid vacations. Self-employed agents must provide these for themselves.

Earnings for travel agents who own their agencies depend mainly on commissions from airlines and other carriers, cruise lines, tour operators, and lodging places. Commissions for domestic travel arrangements, cruises, hotels, sightseeing tours, and car rentals are about 10 percent of the total sale; for international travel, commissions are about 11 percent. They may also charge a service fee for the time and expense involved in planning a trip.

Meet Some Sales Professionals

Meet Marty Gorelick

Marty Gorelick has a bachelor of arts degree and eight years of experience in computer hardware sales. He has also attended seminars from all of the major computer manufacturers: Compaq, IBM, Hewlett Packard, Sony, Apple, and NEC. He is account manager for county government sales at GE Capital IT Solutions in Miami, Florida, where he services Metro-Dade, Broward, and Pasco Counties plus all cities, towns, and villages within these municipalities.

"The computer industry is constantly changing," he says. "It is the fastest-growing industry in the world. Every person on our planet is connected in one way or another. Computers have made communications possible at lightning speed.

"Scientists, doctors, engineers, lawyers, manufacturers, teachers, those in the arts, and every other element of our society operates at higher levels of proficiency than ever before because of computers. For example, a doctor in Seattle can supervise a surgical procedure in an operating room located in Atlanta through the aid of a computer hookup. Ten short years ago, this was impossible. Using a process called Computer Aided Design (CAD), engineers can design structures that will withstand stress far beyond their intended safety limits. Police can track known law offenders well outside of their jurisdiction and notify other law enforcement officers of potential problems. This, by far, is only the tip of the iceberg. Computer applications are endless.

"A typical day for me begins when I arrive at my office about 6:30 A.M. After running the branch's allocation reports for all the salespeople in our office, I check my voice mail for any emergency issues that must be addressed quickly. An example might be a critical shipment that hasn't arrived on time or a file server that has developed a problem and is inoperable. These situations demand my immediate attention. If both these situations exist, I'll contact our Atlanta facility to run a tracer and our service department to check out the server on the first call of the day.

"I read my E-mail messages next. It's not unusual to have between five and fifteen messages ranging from company updates to manufacturer price changes to additions and deletions from

any number of vendors. Since I give my E-mail address to my customers, I might see a request for a quotation on a product or clar-
ification of a service agreement or a question about the
configuration of a mini-tower computer with 32MB memory,
2.5GB hard drive and an 8X CD-ROM. Some messages require
a response ASAP; others can be addressed during the course of
my regular business day.

"Next stop is my in-mail box, which usually contains a collection of faxes that have arrived since I left the office at the end of
business yesterday. These faxes could contain purchase orders,
manufacturer promotional notices, seminar information, or news
of a prospective customer looking for a great reseller like ours!
All this, and the clock has not yet struck 8 A.M.

"Now, the doors swing open, and my fellow employees arrive.
The phones go off night ring, and our customers start calling in.
We field calls concerning products, service, availability, addi-
tions, deletions, and changes in orders.

"During the course of the day, the staff may all meet for a
quick meeting to discuss a change in plans concerning a new
company procedure. Our regularly scheduled sales meeting takes
place at 8:30 A.M. sharp each Wednesday. This is when we discuss our progress as a group and host a manufacturer who is
introducing a new product or products.

"We constantly update our price list to remain the most competitive reseller in the marketplace. I do a special electronic price
list for the county every sixty days. This process usually takes me
anywhere from three to four working days. I also provide a man-
uscript of more than five thousand items from a third-party
vendor. On any given day, I may accompany a manufacturer
downtown to the county building, where we will call on a number of departments who have requested information or a demon-
stration of a new item.

"Afternoons are generally reserved for cleaning up all unfin-
ished projects, faxing quotes, looking for odd items that appear
on purchase orders, and filing away POs and invoices. My day

ends about the time that local traffic starts to build on the highway. This represents a ten-plus-hour day, five days a week, four point three weeks a month. To say this is a hectic day is putting it mildly. However, if you enjoy what you do, it can be and *is* a labor of love.

"The most enjoyable part of my position is helping my customers understand their needs in respect to the use of the equipment. An example would be a customer interested in a laptop computer to do presentations at remote sites versus a client needing a laptop for communicating to his home base. One would need a CD-ROM; the other might only need a fax/modem. Some may need both.

"If I had to pick a project I least like to perform, it's the tons of paperwork that is a necessary evil in the day-to-day flow of business. The upsides of my business are the satisfaction of being productive and helping others do the same. When I complete a project with confidence in a timely manner so my customers can enjoy productivity, I take a moment to sit back and breathe easy.

"The downside is always the fact of being in a race with the clock. I try to never let the clock win. I also refuse to let a discontinued product stop me from saying to a customer that I can fill their needs. Somewhere out there is a replacement part. All salespeople are part detective. We look until we find what we need to help our customers.

"For those who are considering entering my world, I would say to be prepared to plan for a very exciting career. Technology advances as fast as you can absorb yesterday's breakthroughs. Pick a school that offers the career path that you wish to follow (sales and marketing, computer network engineering, or service and repair). Attend as many seminars in the field as possible. Read as many journals that pertain to your area of interest. Spend as much time as you can afford, talking to those around you in that particular field. Don't be afraid to roll up your sleeves and get your hands dirty. Ask a million questions. Experiment with the knowledge you've gained. Share your findings with others and never stop learning. That's my formula for success."

Meet Donna Maas

Donna Maas's formal studies include interior architecture, design, drafting, and oil painting. With a background in graphic art, she designs all marketing materials and packaging for MAAS Polishing Systems™ of Willowbrook, Illinois. She serves as president and CEO of the company.

After six years of using various cleaning and polishing products and always wishing for something better, Maas asked a chemist to assist her in formulating a product that worked. The end result is MAAS Polishing Creme, a product that quickly restores metals, fiberglass, Plexiglas, and dull or oxidized paintwork to a brilliant finish. "Little did I realize how this innovative formula would revolutionize the polishing products industry," she says.

"The job is glamorous, hectic, and unpredictable," Maas explains. "My role encompasses product development, designing marketing materials, and fielding calls from major retailers while maintaining balance in the offices, warehouse, and factory. This, combined with extensive traveling and television appearances on QVC to demonstrate my products, requires tremendous stamina. Everyone within the company, from my executive assistant to the shipping department, will tell you that every project I tackle must be treated with urgency, requiring immediate attention. This keeps my office personnel (including myself) operating at an unusually fast pace.

"By the third year in business, I experienced an 800 percent growth on my initial investment," she says. "It is tremendously fulfilling to obtain such rapid success and worldwide recognition. I would have to think long and hard if asked what the downside of my career is because I can't think of anything!

"I would advise others who wish to get into this field to stay focused. The most difficult thing for an entrepreneur to do is to focus. You have so many things coming at you all at once. I have learned to concentrate on the most promising opportunities. When you become scattered and attempt to address every opportunity, your success is hindered."

Meet Jim LeClair

Jim Leclair is the owner and sales manager for Advanced Computer Services in Lawrence, Kansas. He earned a high school
diploma and took some secondary accounting and business
classes. He also has engaged in ongoing seminars and classes that
are offered by suppliers to enhance sales, technical training, and
product knowledge.

"I was burned out on retail and on working for others," he says,
"so my wife and I decided to form our own business. She had a
strong computer background, and I had more of the business
background. We felt our strengths would complement one
another. Our company consists of training and network installa-
tions; network design to integration; support; and fiber optics, to
name a few.

"We have five employees. Our store hours are Monday through
Friday, from 8 A.M. until 5 P.M. The atmosphere is as relaxed as
possible—business casual Monday through Thursday, casual on
Friday. Our busiest time of the year is summer.

"I try to keep politics out of the workplace and am flexible
with my employees and their families as much as possible. Overtime, for instance, is kept to a minimum.

"A day can change within the first five minutes you walk in
the door. You have to be able to juggle things around to grease
the squeakiest wheel. I generally arrive at 7:00 A.M. and leave
between 6:30 and 7:00 P.M., spending approximately 30 percent
of my time administering to the customers needs, 40 percent
working on sales, and 30 percent on day-to-day activities of running the business.

"What I like best is seeing how happy the customer is when we
say this is how the network will work, and then the network performs as well or better than we anticipated. What I like least is
having to discipline employees or contemplate lost sales.

"To be successful in this kind of work, it's very important to
keep abreast of the current technology at all times, to be a good

listener, to be flexible, to be able to read people, and to understand what they really want, not what they say they want. You have to be able to think quickly on your feet and have a semi-aggressive nature. You just can't take no for an answer. Still, you must sell the customers what they want. Don't try to sell people something that isn't right for them, just because you can make some money.

"I'd advise those who are considering computer sales to be honest, to be fair, and to *always* do a good job. Our business has grown because we have gained the trust of both our customers and our employees."

For More Information

By contacting the following list of professional associations, you can obtain more information about each category of sales.

Retail Sales

Information on careers in retail sales may be obtained from the personnel offices of local stores, from state merchants' associations, or from local unions of the United Food and Commercial Workers International Union.

In addition, general information about retailing is available from:

National Retail Federation
701 Pennsylvania Avenue NW
Washington, DC 20004-2608

Services Sales

For details about employment opportunities for services sales representatives, contact employers who sell services in your area.

For information on careers and scholarships in hotel management and sales, contact:

The American Hotel and Motel Association (AH&MA)
Information Center
1201 New York Avenue NW
Washington, DC 20005-3931

Manufacturing and Wholesale Sales

Information on manufacturers' agents is available from:

Sales and Marketing Management International
Statler Office Tower
Cleveland, OH 44115

Insurance Sales

General occupational information about insurance agents and brokers is available from the home office of many life and casualty insurance companies. Information on state licensing requirements may be obtained from the department of insurance at any state capital.

Information about a career as a life insurance agent also is available from:

National Association of Life Underwriters
1922 F Street NW
Washington, DC 20006

For information about insurance sales careers in independent agencies and brokerages, contact:

National Association of Professional Insurance Agents
400 North Washington Street
Alexandria, VA 22314

For information about professional designation programs, contact:

American Society of CLU and ChFC
270 Bryn Mawr Avenue
Bryn Mawr, PA 19010-2195

Society of Certified Insurance Counselors
3630 North Hills Drive
Austin, TX 78731

Society of Chartered Property and Casualty Underwriters
Kahler Hall
720 Providence Road
P.O. Box 3009
Malvern, PA 19355-0709

Real Estate Sales

Details on licensing requirements for real estate agents, brokers, and appraisers are available from most local real estate and appraiser organizations or from the state real estate commission or board.

For more information about opportunities in real estate work, contact:

National Association of Realtors
777 Fourteenth Street NW
Washington, DC 20005

Information on careers and licensing and certification requirements in real estate appraising is available from:

American Society of Appraisers
P.O. Box 17265
Washington, DC 20041

Appraisal Institute
875 North Michigan Avenue, Suite 2400
Chicago, IL 60611-1980

Travel Agents

For information on careers in the travel industry, contact:

American Society of Travel Agents
1101 King Street
Alexandria, VA 22314

Association of Retail Travel Agents
1745 Jefferson Davis Highway, Suite 300
Arlington, VA 22202

Institute of Certified Travel Agents
148 Linden Street
P.O. Box 56
Wellesley, MA 02181

CHAPTER THREE

Careers in Marketing, Advertising, and Public Relations

"Good times, bad times, there will always be advertising. In good times people want to advertise; in bad times they have to."
BRUCE BURTON, *Town and Country*

W ell before the sales team hits the road with its merchandise or services, another team of professionals—product developers and experts in marketing, advertising, public relations, and publicity—must perform its duties first.

The goal of marketing is to reach the consumer—to motivate or persuade a potential buyer; to sell a product, service, idea, or cause; to gain political support; or to influence public opinion.

The fundamental objective of any firm is to market its products or services profitably. To do so, an overall marketing policy must be established, including product development, market research, market strategies, sales approaches, advertising outlets, promotion possibilities, and effective pricing and packaging.

Marketing executives determine the demand for products and services offered by the firm and its competitors and identify potential consumers, such as business firms, wholesalers, retailers, government, or the general public. Mass markets are further categorized according to various factors, such as region, age, income, and lifestyle.

In small firms, all marketing responsibilities may be assumed by the owner or chief executive officer. In large firms, which may offer numerous products and services nationally or even world-wide, experienced professionals working together coordinate these and related activities.

Marketing

In simple terms, salespeople try to encourage people to buy what they are selling, and marketers try to figure out what consumers have a need for. Marketers start at the beginning of the cycle and look at the customer, asking themselves, "I wonder what they need." Once that is determined, marketers look at their company and ask themselves, "Do we know how to produce it and can we make money doing it?"

The Steps Involved

Once marketers come up with a product idea (the ideas might come from talking to customers or during brainstorming sessions) they start communicating with the product development department, which in some industries might be scientists or engineers. They form a team that includes marketing management, marketing researchers, engineers, advertisers, a financial advisor, and eventually salespeople.

First the team must decide if the product idea is something their customers really want. This is called market research. Market researchers set up focus groups, bringing a group of customers together and talking to them to find out what isn't working in their present environment and what they truly need.

Professionals working in market research departments are tuned in to the consumer—what he or she worries about, desires, thinks, believes, and holds dear. Market researchers conduct surveys or one-on-one interviews, utilize existing research, test consumer reactions to new products or advertising copy, track sales figures and buying trends, and become overall experts on consumer behavior.

Agency research departments can design questionnaires or other methods of studying groups of people, implement the surveys, and interpret the results. Sometimes research departments hire an outside market research firm to take over some of the workload. For example, a market researcher could come up with a procedure to test the public's reaction to a television commercial; the outside firm could put the procedure into action.

Marketing research assistants report directly to a research executive and are responsible for compiling and interpreting data and monitoring the progress of research projects.

After the market research is conducted, marketers attempt to quantify that need in the marketplace. If thirty people have told them they need a particular device, that suggests a strong need, but the company can't afford to build something for just thirty people. It wants to make sure there are enough people out there willing to buy the product. This sparks another round of research.

With successful research results, the concept development stage begins. This is the development of a word or paragraph that describes the product. In some instances, marketers then take that to engineers who develop a prototype. The prototype is taken to the marketplace for testing and evaluations. With feedback in hand, the team begins to make product improvements.

Once company officials are at least 95 percent sure this is the product they want, they give it a final test in the marketplace. They also test for claims. For example, a company might want to claim that their new hospital bed will prevent skin sores, but they need to be able to document that claim.

If all test results point to being able to move forward, the engineers start figuring out how to mass produce the product, and marketers plan how their company can make money on it. For that, they have to look at the production cost and how much customers would be willing to pay for it. One of the big misconceptions in this area is that you take the cost and add a profit percentage to it. Cost is not determined that way. It is determined by what people are willing to pay.

The next step is promotion planning. Now that the company has a product, it has to find a way to get the word out. The appropriate team members make brochures and design advertising. At the same time, the numbers are being crunched and production schedules are being set up. Marketing experts need to know how fast the product can be made, how fast it can get out to the field, how many will be bought, and how big the profit will be.

Once a date is set for introducing the product, the sales force is brought in and taught how to present it. Then the product is monitored to see if it's meeting its sale projections. If it's not making the projected numbers, top management wants to know why and what is going to be done about it. Often though, if it is making the numbers or doing better, top management still wants to know why. That's the way it goes in a competitive business.

Job Settings for Marketing Professionals

Marketing professionals are found in virtually every industry. Industries employing them in significant numbers include motor vehicle dealers, printing and publishing firms, department stores, computer and data processing services firms, management and public relations firms, and advertising agencies.

Because marketers and advertising professionals work hand in hand, many marketing departments are located within corporate advertising departments or within private advertising agencies. Private marketing firms function similarly to advertising agencies and work toward the same goals—identifying and targeting specific audiences that will be receptive to specific products, services, or ideas.

Experts advise that you start your job search before you near graduation. Those who arrange internships for themselves have an edge; they've already become familiar faces on the job. When an opening comes up, a known commodity (who performed well during the internship) is going to be chosen over an unknown one. Learn as much as you can about the agency or firm you're interested in. In other words, target your prospects.

Working Conditions

Marketers work long hours, often including evenings and weekends. Working under pressure is unavoidable as schedules change, problems arise, and deadlines and goals must be met.

Marketing managers meet frequently with other managers; some meet with the public and government officials. Substantial travel may be involved. For example, attendance at meetings sponsored by associations or industries is often mandatory.

The Downsides

Although marketing is considered by many to be a "step up" from sales, there's a downside to it. If the company is not making the expected profit, marketers could easily lose their jobs. Their responsibilities for sales volume and profit are the same as those for salespeople.

In essence, marketers make an agreement with sales. For example, they think, "OK, we are going to sell one hundred units of X product to a particular customer." But if they spend too much money in product development or advertising and then sell only ninety units (though the salesperson has the first responsibility), marketers are also responsible. They had agreed on what could be sold with specific advertising and on setting a certain price. If the mark is missed, marketing jobs are also on the line.

Another downside is that marketers usually supervise salespeople, but the sales force often makes more money than the marketers do—possibly a lot more money. But, to make up for it, marketers usually also receive a good pension plan and bonuses.

Marketing is a very competitive field, but as a competitive spirit, you wouldn't have it any other way.

Training for Marketing Professionals

A wide range of educational backgrounds are suitable for entry into marketing jobs, but many employers prefer a broad liberal arts background. A bachelor's degree in sociology, psychology, literature, or philosophy, among other subjects, is acceptable. However, requirements vary depending upon the particular job.

Most marketing positions are filled by promoting experienced sales and technical personnel, such as sales representatives, purchasing agents, buyers, product or brand specialists, advertising specialists, promotion specialists, and public relations specialists. The best marketers have a dual background, including sales experience and a formal education, ideally an M.B.A. Some start off in sales first, then after being on the job for a while, they go back to school for their master's before moving into marketing.

For marketing management positions, some employers prefer a bachelor's or master's degree in business administration with an emphasis on marketing. Courses in business law, economics, accounting, finance, mathematics, and statistics are also recommended.

In highly technical industries, such as computer and electronics manufacturing, a bachelor's degree in engineering or science, combined with a master's degree in business administration, may be preferred. Familiarity with computerized word processing and database applications is also important.

People interested in becoming marketing managers should be mature, creative, highly motivated, resistant to stress, and flexible, yet decisive. The ability to communicate persuasively, both orally and in writing, with other managers, staff, and the public is vital. Marketing managers also need tact, good judgment, and exceptional ability to establish and maintain effective personal relationships with supervisory and professional staff members and client firms.

Getting Ahead

Because of the importance and high visibility of their jobs, marketing personnel often are prime candidates for advancement. Well-trained, experienced, successful managers may be promoted to higher positions in their own or other firms. Some become top executives. Managers with extensive experience and sufficient capital may open their own businesses.

In small firms, where the number of positions is limited, advancement to a management position may come slowly. In large firms, promotion may occur more quickly.

Although experience, ability, and leadership are emphasized for promotion, advancement may be accelerated by participation in management training programs conducted by many large firms. Many firms also provide their employees with continuing education opportunities, either in-house or at local colleges and universities, and encourage employee participation in seminars and conferences, often provided by professional societies.

Numerous marketing and related associations sponsor national or local management training programs, often in collaboration with colleges and universities. Courses include brand and product management, international marketing, sales management evaluation, telemarketing and direct sales, promotion, marketing communication, market research, organizational communication, and data processing systems procedures and management. Many firms pay all or part of the cost for those who successfully complete courses.

Some associations offer certification programs for marketing managers. (The names and addresses are provided at the end of this chapter.) Certification is a sign of competence and achievement in this field.

While relatively few marketing managers currently are certified, the number of managers who seek certification is expected to grow. For example, Sales and Marketing Executives International offers a management certification program based on education and job performance. The American Marketing Association is developing a certification program for marketing managers.

Earnings for Marketing Professionals

According to the most recent National Association of Colleges and Employers survey, starting salaries for marketing majors graduating in 1997 averaged about $29,000. The median annual salary of marketing managers was $46,000 in 1996. The lowest 10 percent earned $23,000 or less, while the top 10 percent earned $97,000 or more. Many earned bonuses equal to 10 percent or more of their salaries.

Surveys show that salary levels vary substantially depending upon the level of managerial responsibility, length of service, education, and the employer's size, location, and industry. For example, manufacturing firms generally pay marketing managers higher salaries than nonmanufacturing firms.

According to a 1996 survey by *Advertising Age* magazine, the average annual salary of a vice president in marketing was $133,000. Other surveys show a salary range of $25,000 to $250,000 for marketing managers, depending on the level of education, experience, industry, and the number of employees he or she supervises.

Advertising

"The breakfast of champions," "When it rains, it pours," "Where's the beef?"—such phrases are familiar to most of us because of the effective work that advertising specialists have been performing for years. Some consider this phenomenon a nuisance that interrupts television programming and encourages people to buy products that may or may not be best for them. Others look upon it as a great public service. A dominating force in our society, mass media advertising is a multimillion dollar industry dating back to the invention of movable type in the mid-1400s.

Advertising Agencies

Virtually every type of business makes use of advertising in some form, often through the services of an advertising agency. The American Association of Advertising Agencies (the 4As) defines an advertising agency as "a service company that earns its income from planning, creating, producing, and placing printed advertisements and broadcast commercials for its clients." Agencies may also offer additional services, such as market research, sales promotion, television programming, and public relations.

Agencies that are diversified and handle many kinds of advertising are called full-service advertising agencies. Other more specialized agencies may handle only one area, such as direct marketing.

An advertising agency may consist of only one employee or perhaps several thousand. Salaries will tend to be higher for those employed at bigger full-service agencies, because plum accounts like IBM or Pepsi Cola are more likely to engage larger advertising agencies.

Many people think the world of advertising is glamorous and exciting—and certain aspects can be. However, as Karen Cole Winters explains in *Your Career in Advertising*, "If you go into advertising expecting a constant whirl of fun and excitement, you'll probably be disappointed."

The work at each agency is frequently divided among several individuals or departments.

- *Account executives* make sure that clients' work is completed satisfactorily and on time. Account executives must be savvy about their agencies and aware of each client's desires and needs. Their responsibilities lie more in the business arena rather than in the creative aspects of the business.

- *Art directors* must be able to effectively present a theme or idea in convincing visual form, through illustration color, photography, or cinematography.

- *Creative directors* supervise all employees and oversee all activities in the agency. At the top of the hierarchy, creative directors must, of course, be creative and possess people skills and solid business acuity.

- *Researchers* seek to determine what kind of audience would be interested in a particular product or service, why they are interested in the product, and how the public is reacting to advertising campaigns already in place.

- *Media people* work in the department that ensures that commercials are aired on radio and television and that ads get into magazines and newspapers.

Other advertising positions include television producers, print production managers, graphic artists, illustrators, photographers, freelance writers, print production personnel, and traffic managers.

Advertising Copywriters

Advertising copywriters are the real creative force behind advertising campaigns. They dream up the words for commercials and advertisements and conjure up the themes for advertising campaigns. Copywriters may also be responsible for articles about products or services, sales promotion materials, public relations items, billboards, and promotional brochures.

Copywriters usually begin by meeting with the client and/or account executive. After gathering as much information as possible, they let their imaginations flow while looking for a slant on why a product or service is different from all others of its kind. Then they proceed to launch a new advertising campaign with their innovative ideas.

Training for Advertising Specialists

Most employers expect applicants to have college degrees. For those who aspire to become account executives, an M.B.A. is especially important. Many schools offer programs in advertising, and a number of top advertising agencies offer in-house training programs for copywriters and account managers.

Since copywriters deal with a wide cross section of ideas and concepts, a general liberal arts background in combination with business is particularly valued. Courses in such subjects as economics, history, journalism, marketing, advertising, math, social sciences, speech, literature, business administration, human relations, and creative writing are recommended.

Copywriters need the skills that all writers should have—the ability to produce clear, concise prose. Therefore, writing experience in the form of published articles; participation in school, church, or yearbook publications; work for local newspapers or radio or television studios; and internships are all worthwhile endeavors.

Candidates should prepare a portfolio containing three ads from two or three previous advertising campaigns. These can be class assignments or real ads from actual clients. If you have no advertising experience at all, present potential employers with samples of your published writing.

Earnings for Advertising Specialists

There is a considerable range of salaries in this field, particularly in different regions of the country. The median annual salary in advertising agencies is about $35,000. Junior copywriters may start out with as little as $15,000; writers with senior status may earn $50,000 to $100,000 and even more as creative directors.

The larger the agency or account, the higher the salary will be. The best locations for jobs are in large cities such as New York, Chicago, Detroit, Boston, Atlanta, Dallas, Minneapolis, and Los Angeles.

Public Relations

The concept of public relations is definitely not a new invention. It dates back to 1787, during the time of the Constitutional Convention. And in the 1800s, both the North and the South made use of the media during the Civil War in an attempt to persuade the populace to adopt their way of thinking.

The goal of public relations remains the same: to sway the public in a particular direction or to build, maintain, and promote positive relationships between the agencies (or companies) and the public.

Public relations professionals may be self-employed or hired by public relations companies. They may also find work in the PR departments of political parties, nonprofit organizations, hospitals, colleges and universities, trade unions, financial institutions, social service organizations, or clothing companies.

Business and industry rely on corporate public relations to educate the public about their products and services. And since nonprofit organizations do not generally advertise, they count on public service announcements provided by public relations professionals to get their messages out.

The work of a public relations practitioner falls into six main categories:

1. *Research.* This includes all of the preliminary work undertaken to ascertain the client's goals so that a plan to achieve them can be devised. Library research, client

interviews, surveys, opinion polls, and collecting data are all part of this.

2. *Program work.* Once research is completed, a plan is set up based upon the findings.

3. *Writing and editing.* This may come in the form of press releases, presentations to clients, internal memos, reports, and magazine articles.

4. *Special events.* Included in this category are press conferences, special appearances, and autograph signings. All are carefully orchestrated to gain the greatest amount of attention.

5. *Media placement.* It is important to select the most important information to release, choose a good time to release it, and send it to the most advantageous receiver.

6. *Fund-raising.* Fund-raising is what sustains nonprofit organizations. Possible events include membership drives, direct solicitation, and benefit banquets.

Those who work as generalists in the field must be able to perform a wide array of duties at the same time. On any given week they may write press releases for one client, design a brochure for another, approach an editor for a third, meet with a talk show host for a fourth, implement a promotion for a fifth, set up a press conference for a sixth, put together a press kit for a seventh, work out the beginnings of a client contact for an eighth, and field media questions for a ninth!

In the governmental arena, public relations specialists may be called press secretaries, communications specialists, or information officers. A senator's press secretary informs the elected official's constituents of his or her accomplishments and responds to questions from the media and the press. The press secretary schedules and appears at press conferences and issues statements from his or her superior.

Training for Public Relations Personnel

Although there is no defined training program for public relations specialists, it is wise to combine a bachelor's degree with some public relations experience, particularly in the form of internships. Professionals in this field often have college majors in journalism, advertising, public relations, or communications. Some companies express a preference for someone with an M.B.A.

Typical courses include public relations principles and techniques; public relations management and administration, including organizational development; writing, emphasizing news releases, proposals, annual reports, scripts, speeches, and related items; visual communications, including desktop publishing and computer graphics; and research, emphasizing social science research and survey design and implementation.

Earnings for Public Relations Personnel

Median yearly earnings for full-time public relations specialists average about $32,000. A recent College Placement Council salary survey found that new college graduates entering the public relations field were offered an average beginning salary of $21,000. According to a recent salary survey by the Public Relations Journal, public relations managers averaged $44,000.

In the federal government, individuals with bachelor's degrees start at about $23,000; with master's degrees, $28,000. Those in managerial positions average about $46,000. A press secretary's salary will generally fall between $20,000 and $70,000.

Meet Some Professionals

Meet Tracy Larrua

Tracy Larrua is a senior account executive for Macy & Associates, a public relations firm based in Venice, California. Larrua attended a performing arts high school, then entered business college, but she ended up working at an advertising agency instead of getting her degree. She worked her way up the ladder in advertising after six years with a company called Ogilvie and Mather. She then began doing public relations work, which she has been doing now for the past twelve years.

"My typical day is spent writing pitch letters, developing story ideas for editors, adding/deleting/updating our media database to be as up-to-date as possible as to what is going on with our clients," says Larrua. "While wearing a headset, I also make a lot of phone calls. The atmosphere is never relaxed. Actually, it is usually very high stress—but it's a fun stress. Our typical work week is a forty-plus week, but depending on client demand, workload, and editorial deadlines, it can easily turn into a sixty-plus week.

"Our company has the coolest environment," she says happily. "We operate from an old two-story brick firehouse that contains off-white walls with no offices, but separate working areas. My space is a room with a view and two big windows that let in fresh air. The space is definitely very interactive. We have no doors. There are high ceilings and a very artsy conference room and lots of natural light. Whenever clients or friends come by, they tell us our offices look like high-tech office space. We also play music throughout the day, and it's probably the most enjoyable and productive office environment I've ever had the pleasure of working in.

"The people I work with are great. Each of us brings different strengths to the group and our personalities complement one another. That's key when you work in a smaller office environment. The only downside is that our company specializes in public relations for real estate and architectural clients. I enjoy this but I'd like to bring in more consumer-type clients in the future—like restaurants, hotels, travel accounts.

"I would recommend that others who are interested in entering this profession get in on the ground floor and act like a sponge. Soak up everything you can," she stresses. "As you start developing your skills, you'll find yourself ascending. Also, stay flexible. This industry has gone through all sorts of changes. Learn, adapt, and adopt a fearless attitude."

Larrua also adds a word of caution— "If you aren't the 'people type,' don't even consider getting into this business. You have to be comfortable and persuasive in talking to people—all kinds of people. Remember—your personality skills account for a lot in this industry."

Meet Betsy Nichol

Betsy Nichol heads her own public relations agency, Nichol & Company of New York. She earned a bachelor of science in journalism from Boston University and has continued to enhance her credentials through seminars and professional workshops.

"I started my career as a journalist, as many public relations experts do," Nichol says. "I was lucky enough to serve a three-month internship at Fairchild Publications and then a full-time position with one of their (then) daily newspapers —*Home Furnishings Daily* (now *HFN*). After three and a half years there, I was recruited by a small public relations firm. Early on in my career, someone told me I should have my own business, and at the time I thought he was crazy, but as the years went by I realized that I'm one of those people who is better at being my own boss than working for someone else.

"I was attracted to the field because of the fast pace and the realization that no two days would be alike. I knew I would always be learning about different subjects and meeting interesting people from all types of professions.

"I also like to communicate in writing, and good writing skills are essential in the PR business. There's never a dull moment in this business and being successful requires many of the same skills as being a journalist. It's been an exciting journey.

"Being head of a public relations firm is very hectic," Nichol stresses. "The phone is always ringing—and you never know if it's a client with a crisis, an editor on a deadline, or an employee with a question.

"The public relations business is filled with deadlines and curveballs. As the head of the agency, I spend a lot of time in meetings with clients or counseling them by phone and meeting with employees to guide their progress in achieving client objectives. Other time is spent on new business activities, keeping up with industry trends, and making internal changes accordingly. Much of my time is also spent on the endless administrative tasks involved in running a business.

"I'm continually monitoring my E-mail, talking on the phone, giving instructions to staffers, and receiving countless faxes, notes, and mailed items that require a quick response. There is never enough time in a day.

"Networking is also important for success. I attend and speak at many meetings, workshops, breakfasts, and lunches that can produce new business, provide insight into industry trends, and form strategic alliances that enable me to serve my clients better.

"The public relations business offers endless ways to express one's creativity. It also demands that one think strategically to help clients solve their problems, which keeps me on my toes and makes every day action packed.

"In running a business of twelve people, there is also a great sense of teamwork and caring among the staffers—not a typical office environment. The interaction between us produces exciting results and great fun. The downside is that we often have to cancel evening plans and work late to meet breaking deadlines.

"My advice to others who are considering this field is to work hard, be flexible and both patient and impatient in your quest for success."

Meet Edward Pitkoff

Edward Pitkoff, of Omaha, Nebraska, attended the Philadelphia Museum School of Art, the Pennsylvania Academy of Fine Arts,

Temple University, and Studio School of Art and Design, all in Philadelphia, Pennsylvania. He also attended a wide variety of marketing and advertising seminars and the School of Visual Arts in New York for a course in television production and direction. He has held several high-ranking positions in marketing, advertising, and sales and is founder and president of Creative Decisions, Inc., of New York.

"My career began in 1961," says Pitkoff. "After twelve years in positions of designer, assistant art director, art director, and creative director, a freelance business presented itself, and I formed Ed Pitkoff Studios. This expanded and evolved into Creative Decisions, Inc., in 1973, and there the story truly started.

"The idea of doing high-quality creative advertising that could convince a consumer to purchase a product was very attractive to me. Early on, one thing that had a profound effect on me was having a mentor who taught me how to marry the communication to the consumer so that the buyer could visualize themselves as part of the product.

"Don't ever become distracted," says Pitkoff. "Always keep your focus on the business of advertising. And remember—what *you* might want to say to sell this product or service really isn't important. The only thing that *is* important is what would be compelling to the consumer. What do they want to hear? What do they want to buy? Ultimately, it is the consumer who is the judge of how well your message has come across. If the product sells, then you know your focused communication has reached its audience."

Meet Dennis Abelson

Dennis Abelson earned a bachelor of arts degree in classical languages from Washington University in St. Louis and subsequently earned a master of science in journalism, specializing in advertising, from Northwestern Medill School of Communications in Evanston, Illinois. He has experience as a copywriter, associate creative director, and creative director.

"Ten years ago I was making a substantial living as a freelance writer," he says. "But the isolation and lack of significant, bigger-budget creative challenges was starting to bring me down. Then I was contacted by Don Tomala, my future partner, who had come across one of my promotional mailings. He was in the process of establishing an integrated, full-service marketing consulting and communications firm to fill a gap he had experienced as a Fortune 500 sales and marketing director. After a somewhat rocky start (it was the middle of an economic recession, and few companies had even heard of integrated marketing), we eventually bootstrapped ourselves into a successful, growing company. Two years ago, Tomala and I disassociated ourselves from a third partner and changed our corporate name from The Figa Group to Matrix Partners.

"Our current client roster is comprised of a highly eclectic mix of companies that turn to us for a wide range of services, including packaging, advertising, promotions, direct mail, and sales presentations. In 1997, we became the agency of record for Anixter International, a global distributor of computer cabling and networking systems. We also serve the Quaker Oats Continental Coffee Division, the American National Can Flexible Packaging Group, Vitner's Potato Chips, the Dive Equipment and Marketing Association, and MS BioScience, a fast-growing agricultural biotech company.

"I originally got into the creative end of advertising because I couldn't see myself holding down a nine-to-five job. It also gave me the opportunity to keep pursuing my interests in audio engineering and cartooning. In my undergraduate years, I was program director of the campus radio station as well as the creator of a weekly comic strip in the campus paper.

"There is no typical day in this industry, which is why it attracts so many people. But it might unfold somewhat like this:

8:00 to 9:00 A.M.—Revise ad copy, circulate for internal review.

9:00 to 10:00 A.M.—Project status meetings, logistics, costs.

10:00 to 10:30 A.M.—Finalize ad copy and fax to client.

10:30 to 11:00 A.M.—Review logo designs and alternate color treatments for new brand.

11:00 to 12:00 P.M.—Perform on-line trademark search for proposed theme line.

12:00 to 1:00 P.M.—Have lunch at desk while drafting new business presentation.

1:00 to 1:30 P.M.—Call client regarding new promotion.

1:30 to 4:00 P.M.—Conceptualize with designer and writer on direct-mail project.

4:00 to 4:30 P.M.—Attend internal meeting to refine thinking on new business presentation.

4:30 to 5:00 P.M.—Edit PC-based presentation for biotech client.

5:00 to 6:00 P.M.—Finalize new business presentation.

6:00 to 7:00 P.M.—Continue conceptualizing on direct-mail project; take home to finish.

9:00 to 11:00 P.M.—Finish writing direct mailer.

"What does it mean to be doing my kind of work?" asks Abelson. "At times it seems totally thankless, but in what other profession do you get paid to legally hallucinate, to play creatively with concepts and pictures? Here is my list of 'upsides':

- No time for corporate politics or hidden agendas

- The opportunity to be knowledgeable with more than a hundred different industries

- The satisfaction of contributing visibly and dramatically to the success of a client's business

"And here are the 'downsides':

- The hours

- Certain clients who shall remain nameless

- Certain clients who play it safe when they should be competing

- Logistical and budgetary constraints on creativity

"I would tell others who are considering a career in advertising and marketing to start with the largest organization that will hire them. And be prepared for the long haul."

Meet Joanne Levine

Joanne Levine's company, Chicago-area-based Lekas & Levine Public Relations Inc., specializes in pursuing media publicity for small and midsize businesses. "Media public relations is probably the most popular among clients," says Levine, "but it is also the most stressful for the practitioner. Although I also write copy for brochures and business letters and plan some special events, 80 percent of my time is spent trying to help my clients make the news—that is, helping them to appear in newspapers, magazines, and trade publications and on radio and television. My clients recognize that media publicity is a valuable tool to increase visibility of their products or services, while enhancing their images in the eyes of potential customers, suppliers, business associates, and peers. While paid advertising 'looks like an ad,' editorial appearances add credibility and help to establish the client as an authority in his or her respective field. Whether a fledgling entrepreneur or an established pillar of the business community, there are few people who wouldn't relish the opportunity to make a favorable impression in the news.

"On the other hand, my specialty is probably the least favorite among public relations practitioners. With an ad, you know what day it will appear, what size it will be, and exactly what it will say. With an article, I hold my breath until the client and I read it in the publication. With a taped interview on radio or television, I wait to see if anything was cut or taken out of context. While my press release and phone conversation with an editor might have been chockfull of the kind of information I hope they will relay to the public, there are no guarantees such as those in advertising. I work with editors and writers who are always on deadline, always overworked, but nevertheless always looking for a good angle. For these reasons, my job can be stressful and sometimes plagued with problems that are completely out of my control.

"But when all goes well, there's nothing like it. I have seen the positive results of good, steady media campaigns time and time again. And more than once in a while, a really big media appearance can make an overnight difference in someone's business. The client is on cloud nine, his or her phones begin to ring off the hook with new business, and I am showered with praise and gratitude. I often get to know my clients well and enjoy friendly, upbeat working relationships with them. The knowledge that I am helping to make a client's business grow is very rewarding.

"Although a degree in journalism or communications is certainly desirable, in my particular case, I entered this career without any real planning. Even though I majored in English in college, I didn't really have any ambition to focus on public relations. When my children were babies, I didn't even work outside the home but joined various local community groups, such as Friends of the Parks, the PTA, and a human relations group. In the course of setting up a fund-raiser for one of the organizations, I was paired with a real life PR pro on the publicity committee. She really gave me an education, and I became fascinated with her skills. At the same time, my very creative brother was writing music, forming bands, and starting wacky side businesses. One of his companies created and marketed original adult board games he designed. To test my newfound skills, each time he introduced a game, I sent out press releases to the media. The first game, *Danger Island*, even included me as one of the characters. When the reporters came out, I became part of their story. We got spectacular local and national coverage.

"That first project really whet my appetite. From there, I began publicizing my husband's retail stores, more civic groups, and the like. One day, I thought about the fact that I was doing a great job and not getting paid for it. I recruited my brother's wife to help me, and we wrote a press release about two sisters-in-law who started a public relations company devoted to small businesses. We got an immediate response from the local chain of newspapers. They wrote a feature article about our company, even though we had no clients. The rest, they say, is history. From that initial article, the phone began to ring, and, within a month or two, we had five clients. It's been word of mouth ever since.

"My sister-in-law stayed aboard for nine years and finally decided to go back to her first love, teaching. She always felt that even if she did a great job pitching an idea to an editor, it was always that editor who determined how well we did our job. We were always caught in the middle. If the article was great, the client thought we were, too. If the article was small, all the effort we put into the project seemed insignificant. The stress finally got to her, and she left. I, on the other hand, thrive on the highs and the lows. Not knowing what the day will bring seems exciting to me. One 'yes' from an editor and I'm as happy as a clam.

"If you want a career in media publicity, I would advise you to read, read, read. Study the format of newspapers, watch the twelve, five, six, and ten o'clock news. Read every magazine you can get your hands on and note how things are laid out. Reporters have certain 'beats,' and if you can zero in on what they write about, half the battle is won. Familiarizing oneself with the media is a never-ending responsibility. While there are a few good media guides that provide information, this is not a substitute for studying the style of an individual person, section, or publication. Also, as the media faces the same cutbacks and consolidations as any other industry, changes in personnel happen at a rapid pace.

"If you don't want to go through the trial-and-error process as much as I did, try to get an internship with a PR company. I have used graduate students from the Medill School of Journalism at Northwestern University as freelancers several times. Just remember that in order to make it in this field, you need a good imagination and the ability to find an 'angle.' I can't tell you how many times a client has said, 'I do a better job than anyone else in town and I truly care about my customers.' That's very nice, but it's boring! Find out why the client does a better job. What does he or she do differently? Is the business owner an interesting person? What are his or her hobbies? The list goes on and on. You must be able to pick someone's brain until something newsworthy pops out. Then, you must learn who might be fascinated with your information—so much so that they want to inform their readers about it or share it with their television audience.

"As I look back over the weeks, months, and years, I feel that the most rewarding part of my effort is the knowledge that I have truly made a difference in my clients' businesses and, consequently, in their lives. The wide diversity of my clientele makes for a job that never gets boring. And when I look ahead, more than anything else, I wonder what my next subject will be."

For More Information

The following list includes professional associations and directories that can aid in your job search. Many of the publications are available in public libraries.

The American Marketing Association is a professional society of marketing and market research executives, sales and promotion managers, advertising specialists, academics, and others interested in marketing. The association fosters research; sponsors seminars, conferences, and student marketing clubs; and provides a placement service. It also offers a certification program for marketing managers.

The association publishes the *Journal of Marketing, Journal of Marketing Research, Journal of Health Care Marketing,* and an international membership directory. For more information, contact:

American Marketing Association
250 South Wacker Drive
Chicago, IL 60606

Members in the National Council For Marketing and Public Relations are communications specialists working within community colleges in areas including alumni, community, government, media, public relations, marketing, publications, and coordinating special events. The association works to foster improved relations between two-year colleges and their communities.

They hold an annual conference with exhibits, national surveys, and needs assessment and publish a journal called *Counsel.* For information, contact:

National Council For Marketing and Public Relations
364 North Wyndham Avenue
Greely, CO 80634

Sales and Marketing Executives International offers a management certification program. Additional information can be obtained by contacting:

Sales and Marketing Executives International
458 Statler Office Tower
Cleveland, OH 44115

Magazine Publishing Career Directory
Gale Research, Inc.
P.O. Box 33477
Detroit, MI 48232-5477

CHAPTER FOUR

Careers in Law

"If there were no bad people, there would be no good lawyers."
CHARLES DICKENS, *The Old Curiosity Shop*

I
f you're considering a career as a lawyer, maybe you're holding images of Johnny Cochran or the stars of TV's *Law and Order* or *LA Law*. You probably remember *Perry Mason* or have seen the show's reruns. His clients were always innocent, he always got them off, and he always nabbed the real criminal to boot.

But real life doesn't always follow the imagination of television writers. If criminal law is the area that interests you, you should know that many of your clients will not be innocent, and you might not be able to get them all off. Some you'd even rather not represent. But, in our justice system, everyone is innocent until proven guilty, and everyone is entitled to legal defense.

Areas of Specialty

Criminal law, however, while a very popular and much publicized specialty, is not the only avenue lawyers can pursue. The more detailed aspects of a lawyer's job depend upon his or her field of specialization and position. Even though all lawyers are allowed to represent parties in court, some appear in court more frequently than others. Some lawyers specialize in trial work. These lawyers need an exceptional ability to think quickly and speak with ease and authority and must be thoroughly familiar with courtroom rules and strategy. But trial lawyers still spend most of their time outside the courtroom conducting research, interviewing clients and witnesses, and handling other details in preparation for trial.

Besides trials, attorneys may specialize in other areas. Some may never see the inside of a courtroom. The majority of lawyers are in private practice where they may concentrate on criminal or civil law. What follows is an overview of each type of law specialization.

Criminal Law

In criminal law, lawyers represent people who have been charged with crimes. Their responsibility is to argue their cases in courts of law. Criminal lawyers operate their own practices, work for private law firms, or represent clients under the auspices of the public defender's office.

Lawyers who work for state attorneys, general prosecutors, and courts play a key role in the criminal justice system. At the federal level, attorneys investigate cases for the Department of Justice or other agencies. Also, lawyers at every government level help develop programs, draft laws, interpret legislation, establish enforcement procedures, and argue civil and criminal cases on behalf of the government.

Civil Law

In civil law, attorneys assist clients with litigation, wills, trusts, contracts, mortgages, titles, and leases. Some manage personal property as trustees or, as executors, see that provisions of clients' wills are carried out. Others handle only public interest cases, civil or criminal, that have a potential impact extending well beyond the individual client.

Other lawyers work for legal aid societies, private, nonprofit organizations established to serve disadvantaged people. These lawyers generally handle civil rather than criminal cases.

Some other specializations within civil law include:

bankruptcy

probate

international law

environmental law

intellectual property

insurance law

family law

corporate law

real estate law

tax law

Lawyers sometimes are employed full-time by a single client. If the client is a corporation, the lawyer is known as house counsel and usually advises the company about legal questions that arise from its business activities. These questions might involve patents, government regulations, contracts with other companies, property interests, libel issues, or collective bargaining agreements with unions. Some of the entities that employ house counsels are banks and publishing houses.

Government Attorneys

Attorneys employed at the various levels of government make up still another category. The attorney general of any state is the chief law officer of the state. Under the attorney general, you will find hundreds of assistant attorneys general, or district attorneys, as they are often called, in offices in various cities throughout each state.

They represent the state in civil actions—for example, the big tobacco lawsuits that surface in the news from time to time.

In some states, local prosecutors have an appellate division in each office, and these attorneys handle only appeals. Once in a while, one side or the other will request an oral argument, and then the appeals attorneys will have to go to court. If the verdict is overturned, the state often has to retry the case.

Law Clerks

"Law clerk" is a misleading title. Many people mistakenly think it refers to someone who is an administrative assistant as opposed to an attorney. But law clerks are, indeed, full-fledged attorneys. A more fitting job title would be something along the lines of research attorney. Sometimes they're called "elbow clerks" because they work at the elbow of the judge, usually for a one- to two-year stint directly out of law school or, for some, as a full-time, professional career. Duties vary depending on the judge you work with, but often reading briefs, writing notes on them, and conducting research are a law clerk's main responsibilities.

In addition to a law degree, there are other qualifications you should have. Most law clerks have graduated in at least the top quarter or higher of their class. As a full-time career, a job as a law clerk has its pluses and minuses. Salaries are generally much lower than those paid by private law firms, and job security depends on whether the judge you work for stays on the bench. He could retire or fail to win reelection, and then you're out of a job. In contrast, your hours are fairly normal, and there is usually less stress and competition to deal with than in a busy law firm.

Law Professors

A relatively small number of trained attorneys work in law schools. Most are faculty members who specialize in one or more subjects. Others serve as administrators. Some work full-time in nonacademic settings and teach part-time.

Working Conditions for Lawyers

Lawyers spend most of their time in offices, law libraries, and courtrooms. Occasionally a lawyer might meet with a client in his or her home or place of business and, when necessary, in a hospital or prison. They frequently travel to attend meetings; to gather evidence; and to appear before courts, legislative bodies, and other authorities. Salaried lawyers in government and private corporations generally have structured work schedules. Lawyers in private practice may work irregular hours while conducting research, conferring with clients, or preparing briefs during nonoffice hours.

Many specialties require that lawyers work long hours, and about half regularly work fifty hours or more per week. They are under particularly heavy pressure, for example, when a case is being tried. Preparation for court includes keeping abreast of the latest laws and judicial decisions.

Although work generally is not seasonal, the work of tax lawyers and other specialists may be an exception. Lawyers in private practice can often determine their own workload.

The Role of the Attorney

No matter the setting, whether acting as advocates or prosecutors, all attorneys interpret the law and apply it to specific situations. This requires research and communication abilities. Lawyers perform in-depth research into the purposes behind the applicable laws and into judicial decisions that have been applied to those laws under circumstances similar to those currently faced by the client. While all lawyers continue to make use of law libraries to prepare cases, some supplement their search of the conventional printed sources with computer software packages that automatically search the legal literature and identify legal texts that may be relevant to a specific subject.

In litigation that involves many supporting documents, lawyers may also use computers to organize and index the material. Lawyers then communicate the information obtained by research to others.

Training for Lawyers

To practice law in the courts of any state or other jurisdiction, you must be licensed or admitted to its bar. Nearly all states require that applicants for admission to the bar pass a written bar examination. Most jurisdictions also require applicants to pass a separate written ethics examination.

Lawyers who have been admitted to the bar in one jurisdiction occasionally may be admitted to the bar in another without taking an examination if they meet that jurisdiction's standards of good moral character and have a specified period of legal experience. Federal courts and agencies set their own qualifications for those practicing before them.

To qualify for the bar examination in most states, an applicant must complete at least three years of college and graduate from a law school approved by the American Bar Association (ABA) or the proper state authorities.

Seven states accept the study of law in a law office or in combination with study in a law school; only California accepts the study of law by correspondence as qualifying for taking the bar examination.

Several states require registration and approval of students by the State Board of Law Examiners, either before they enter law school or during the early years of legal study. Most beginning lawyers then train with the government or experienced lawyers before they go out on their own. Some join established law firms and work very hard to become partners.

The required college and law school education usually takes seven years of full-time study after high school: four years of undergraduate study, followed by three years in law school. Although some law schools accept a very small number of students after three years of college, most require applicants to have a bachelor's degree.

To meet the needs of students who can attend only part-time, a number of law schools have night or part-time divisions that usually require four years of study. Typical courses for first-year law students include legal history, legal writing, and public speaking. Second- and third-year students typically take criminal law, contract law, corporate law, wills, and real estate law.

Acceptance by most law schools depends on the applicant's ability to show an aptitude for the study of law. This is demonstrated usually through good undergraduate grades, the Law School Admission Test (LSAT) (required by all law schools approved by the American Bar Association), the quality of the applicant's undergraduate school, any prior work experience, and sometimes a personal interview. However, law schools vary in the weight that they place on each of these factors.

Graduates receive the degree of juris doctor (J.D.) or bachelor of law (LL.B.) as the first professional degree. Advanced law degrees may be desirable for those planning to specialize, do research, or teach. Some law students pursue joint degree programs, which generally require an additional year. Joint degree programs are offered in a number of areas, including law and business administration and law and public administration.

Earnings for Lawyers

Law is a much more demanding profession than most people realize, and it is not the high-income profession everyone thinks it is across the board. Yes, there are a lot of attorneys out there earning a lot of money. But there are also attorneys running themselves ragged from courtroom to courtroom and barely earning enough to pay back their school loans.

Contrary to the experience of John Grisham's hero in *The Firm*, annual salaries of beginning lawyers in private industry average about $40,000. But, in some cases, top graduates from the nation's best law schools can start at more than $80,000 a year.

Factors affecting the salaries offered to new graduates include academic record; type, size, and location of employer; and the specialized educational background desired.

Here's a look at average salaries for new law school graduates working for just six months in a variety of specializations:

Private Practice	$50,000
Business/Industry	$45,000
Higher Education	$35,000
Law Clerk	$35,000
Government	$34,500
Public Interest	$30,000

Salaries of experienced attorneys also vary widely according to the type, size, and location of the employer. The average salary of the most experienced lawyers in private industry is more than $134,000, but some senior lawyers who are partners in the nation's top law firms earn more than $1 million annually.

General attorneys in the federal government averaged around $72,700 a year in 1997. The small number of patent attorneys working for the government averaged around $81,600.

Lawyers on salary receive increases as they assume greater responsibilities. Lawyers starting their own practice may need to work part-time in other occupations during the first years to supplement their income. Their incomes usually grow as their practices develop. Lawyers who are partners in law firms generally earn more than those who practice alone.

Meet a Law Professional

Meet Nicole D. Blake

Nicole D. Blake is a self-employed lawyer in Seattle, Washington. She received her bachelor of arts degree in political science from Loyola University in Chicago, then earned her juris doctorate from DePaul University in Chicago.

"I have been a lawyer since 1991," she says. "My first real job out of school was as a public defender. In that capacity, I became involved in dependency law, which is defending parents from losing their rights when the state has removed their kids and put them in foster care. But this was a difficult position because of the high case load. Then I performed some nonlegal work as an adoption social worker for a nonprofit agency for a year and a half. Since I was the last one hired, I was laid off.

"In my private practice, I focus on dependency law, and that has naturally led to family law—divorce, adoption, etc. As a solo practitioner, I enjoy being my own boss, organizing my own schedule. Then again I dislike organizing my own schedule and keeping my own books.

"I always wanted to help others," says Blake. "I don't have a mathematical mind, but I do have a great ability and proclivity for argument, so it seemed an obvious career path. Also, I come from a family that stressed education. Several family members had already followed a career path in law. In fact, one of my cousins was the first blind lawyer admitted to practice in Chicago.

"I rarely know what any given day will really be like. Something unexpected happens every day. Certain responsibilities are constants, however. One activity that usually takes a huge chunk of my day is returning calls. I rarely answer the phone because this is one of the few ways that I can remain in charge of my own time. Another common responsibility is to attend hearings, often in more than one courthouse in more than one city at a time.

Usually I work on at least one legal writing per day. Filing paper-work or figuring out what to do with any certain piece of paper is the time waster that I resent the most.

"I enjoy working with clients, particularly when things are working well. However, I like this aspect of my career less when clients don't understand my role or the abilities (and inabilities) of the law to deal with all of their life issues. Phone calls some-times become oppressive. There are too many. Clients don't always know what is important, so I am swamped.

"I would advise individuals who are interested in getting into law to try debate teams in high school and college. Another bit of advice: study instead of going to parties so that you can get into one of the best possible law schools."

For More Information

The American Bar Association annually publishes *A Review of Legal Education in the United States*, which provides detailed information on each of the 177 law schools approved by the ABA, state requirements for admission to legal practice, a direc-tory of state bar examination administrators, and other informa-tion on legal education. Single copies are free from the ABA, but there is a fee for multiple copies. Free information on the bar examination, financial aid for law students, and law as a career may also be obtained from:

Member Services
American Bar Association
541 North Fairbanks Court
Chicago, IL 60611-3314

Association of American Law Schools
1201 Connecticut Avenue NW, Suite 800
Washington, DC 20036

Information on the LSAT, the Law School Data Assembly
Service, applying to law school, and financial aid for law students
may be obtained from:

Law School Admission Services
P.O. Box 40
Newtown, PA 18940

The specific requirements for admission to the bar in a particular state or other jurisdiction may also be obtained at the state
capitol, from the clerk of the state supreme court, or from the
administrator of the State Board of Bar Examiners.

CHAPTER FIVE

Careers in Research

"Any sufficiently advanced technology is indistinguishable from magic." ARTHUR C. CLARKE, *The Lost Worlds of 2001*

Research Careers in the Biological and Medical Sciences

Many biological scientists and virtually all medical scientists work in the area of research and development. Some conduct basic research to increase our knowledge of living organisms. Others, in applied research, use knowledge provided by basic research to develop new medicines, increase crop yields, and improve the environment. Biological and medical scientists who conduct research usually work in laboratories using electron microscopes, computers, thermal cyclers, and a wide variety of other equipment. Some professionals may conduct experiments on laboratory animals or greenhouse plants. A number of biological scientists perform a substantial amount of research outside of laboratories. For example, a botanist may do research in tropical rain forests to see what plants grow there, or an ecologist may study how a forest area recovers after a fire.

Some biological and medical scientists work in management or administration. They may plan and administer programs for testing foods and drugs, for example, or direct activities at zoos or botanical gardens. Some biological scientists work as consultants to business firms or to government, while others test and inspect foods, drugs, and other products or write for technical publications. Some work in sales and service jobs for companies who manufacture chemicals or other technical products.

Advances in basic biological knowledge, especially at the genetic and molecular levels, continue to spur the field of biotechnology forward. Using this technology, biological and medical scientists manipulate the genetic material of animals or plants, attempting to make organisms more productive or disease resistant. The first application of this technology occurred in the medical and pharmaceutical areas. Many substances not previously available in large quantities are now beginning to be produced by biotechnological means—some may be useful in treating cancer and other diseases. Advances in biotechnology have opened up research opportunities in almost all areas of biology, including commercial applications in agriculture and the food and chemical industries.

Most biological scientists are further classified by the types of organisms they study or by the specific activities they perform, although recent advances in the understanding of basic life processes at the molecular and cellular levels have blurred some traditional classifications.

Aquatic Biologists

Aquatic biologists study plants and animals that live in water. Marine biologists study saltwater organisms, and limnologists study freshwater organisms. Marine biologists are sometimes erroneously called oceanographers, but oceanography usually refers to the study of the physical characteristics of oceans and the ocean floor.

Biochemists

Biochemists study the chemical composition of living things. They try to understand the complex chemical combinations and reactions involved in metabolism, reproduction, growth, and heredity. Much of the work in biotechnology is done by biochemists and molecular biologists because this technology involves understanding the complex chemistry of life.

Botanists

Botanists study plants and their environments. Some study all aspects of plant life; others specialize in areas such as the identification and classification of plants, the structures and functions of plant parts, the biochemistry of plant processes, the causes and cures of plant diseases, and the geological ancestries of plants.

Microbiologists

Microbiologists investigate the growth and characteristics of microscopic organisms such as bacteria, algae, or fungi. Medical microbiologists study the relationships between organisms and disease or the effects of antibiotics on microorganisms. Other microbiologists may specialize in environmental, food, agricultural, or industrial microbiology; virology (the study of viruses); or immunology (the study of mechanisms that fight infections). Many microbiologists use biotechnology as they advance knowledge of cell reproduction and human disease.

Physiologists

Physiologists study life functions of plants and animals, both in the whole organism and at the cellular or molecular level, under normal and abnormal conditions. Physiologists may specialize in functions such as growth, reproduction, photosynthesis, respiration, or movement or in the physiology of a certain area or system of the organism.

Zoologists

Zoologists study animals—their origins, behaviors, diseases, and life processes. Some experiment with or observe the behaviors of live animals in controlled or natural surroundings, while others dissect dead animals to study their structures. Zoologists are usually identified by the animal group they study, such as ornithologists (birds), mammalogists (mammals), herpetologists (reptiles), and ichthyologists (fish).

Ecologists

Ecologists study the relationships among organisms and between organisms and their environments. They also study the effects of influences such as population size, pollutants, rainfall, temperature, and altitude.

Medical Scientists

Biological scientists who do biomedical research are usually called medical scientists. Medical scientists working on basic research delve into the functioning of normal biological systems in order to understand the causes of and to discover treatments for diseases and other health problems. Medical scientists often try to identify the kinds of changes in cells, chromosomes, or genes that signal the development of medical problems, such as different types of cancer.

After identifying structures of or changes in organisms that provide clues to health problems, medical scientists may then work on the treatment of problems. For example, a medical scientist involved in cancer research might try to formulate a combination of drugs that will lessen the effects of the disease. Medical scientists who have a medical degree might then administer the drugs to patients in clinical trials, monitor their reactions, and observe the results. (Medical scientists who do not have a medical degree normally collaborate with a medical doctor who deals directly with patients.) The medical scientist might then return to the laboratory to examine the results and, if necessary, to adjust the dosage levels to reduce negative side effects or try to induce even better results. In addition to using basic research to develop treatments for health problems, medical scientists attempt to discover ways to prevent health problems from developing, such as affirming the link between smoking and increased risk of lung cancer, or alcoholism and liver disease.

Training for Biological and Medical Scientists

For biological scientists, the Ph.D. degree generally is required for college teaching, independent research, and for advancement to administrative positions. A master's degree is sufficient for some jobs in applied research and for jobs in management, inspection, sales, and service. Some graduates with a bachelor's degree start as biological scientists in testing and inspection or get jobs related to biological science, such as technical sales or service representatives. In some cases, graduates with bachelor's degrees are able to work in a laboratory environment on their own projects, but this is unusual. Some may work as research assistants. Others become biological technicians or medical laboratory technologists. Many with bachelor's degrees in biology enter medical, dental, veterinary, or other health profession schools.

Most colleges and universities offer bachelor's degrees in biological sciences and many offer advanced degrees. Curriculums for advanced degrees often emphasize a subfield such as microbiology or botany, but not all universities offer all curriculums. Advanced degree programs include classroom and fieldwork, laboratory research, and a thesis or dissertation. Biological scientists who have advanced degrees often take temporary postdoctoral research positions that provide specialized research experience.

Biological scientists need to be able to work equally efficiently on their own or as part of a team. In addition, they must be able to communicate clearly and concisely, both orally and in writing. Those in private industry who aspire to management or administrative positions should possess good business skills and be familiar with regulatory issues and marketing and management techniques. Those doing field research in remote areas must have physical stamina.

The Ph.D. degree in a biological science is the minimum education required for prospective medical scientists because the work of medical scientists is almost entirely research oriented. A Ph.D. degree qualifies one to do research on basic life processes or on particular medical problems or diseases and to analyze and interpret the results of experiments on patients. Medical scientists who administer drug or gene therapies to human patients or who otherwise interact medically with patients (such as drawing blood, excising tissue, or performing other invasive procedures) must have a medical degree. It is particularly helpful for medical scientists to earn both Ph.D. and medical degrees.

In addition to a formal education, medical scientists are usually expected to spend several years in postdoctoral positions before they are offered permanent jobs. Postdoctoral work provides valuable laboratory experience, including a background in specific processes and techniques (such as gene splicing) that are transferable to other research projects later on. In some institutions, the postdoctoral position can lead to a permanent position.

Earnings for Biological and Medical Scientists

The National Association of Colleges and Employers reports that starting salaries in private industry average $25,400 for those with bachelor's degrees in biological sciences, $26,900 with master's degrees, and about $52,400 for those earning doctoral degrees. Median annual earnings for biological and life scientists are about $36,300.

In the federal government, general biological scientists in non-supervisory, supervisory, and managerial positions earn an average salary of $52,100; microbiologists average $58,700; ecologists, $52,700; physiologists, $65,900; and geneticists, $62,700.

Meet Some Research Professionals

Meet Amadeo J. Pesce, Ph.D.

Dr. Pesce serves as the director of the toxicology laboratory and professor of experimental medicine at the University of Cincinnati Hospital. He has been associated with the University of Cincinnati for the past twenty-three years.

"I always knew I was interested in medical research," says Dr. Pesce. "So that's where I was focused early on. I earned my undergraduate degree at the Massachusetts Institute of Technology. Then I attended Brandeis University for my graduate degree in biochemistry. My postdoctoral scholarship was at the University of Illinois at Champaign-Urbana.

"To do this kind of work, you need to have Ph.D. credentials. I also have board certification from the American Board for Clinical Chemistry, which I think is very important. (Certification is given to those who have the proper scientific background—five years of experience in the field and successful completion of an examination.)

"In my present position, most of the time I work as part of a team of researchers. The composition of the team may change depending on the project. Participants may include postdoctoral fellows, part-time or full-time technologists, pathologists, mathematicians, psychiatrists, substance abuse counselors, and other health and scientific professionals.

"Usually there are several projects going on at the same time. For instance, we're now helping with the clinical trials in developing methods of measurement for a couple of different projects. One project is to help pace patients by monitoring the effectiveness of the drug called AZT, which is used in the treatment of AIDS. We've developed the technology to measure the concentration of drugs inside the cell and are working very closely with the clinician and the clinical trials that are being conducted.

"Another project we're participating in is the study of developing agents that will help combat substance abuse by reducing the craving and the other aspects that make people want to continue to use drugs. In this project, we work with a group of psychiatrists and substance abuse counselors, and they provide specimens from the patients for us to monitor.

"In addition to the hours spent in the laboratory, a considerable portion of my time is spent thinking and writing. One must think things through and be able to communicate them effectively and efficiently in order for the research to have meaning. And, as I convey to my students, if it's not written down, it was never done.

"As an administrator, I have other responsibilities. I supervise a postdoctoral fellow and handle personnel issues and administrative problems. And at this point in my life, I accomplish this and keep fairly regular working hours. But when I was younger (and for many years), I worked from seven in the morning until ten at night, five days a week. The other two days, I only worked eight to ten hours a day. This was not required, but just my own enthusiasm showing, based upon my decision to be one of the four most recognized authorities in the field. So I set on a path of learning all I could and then proceeded to put out a series of books (eighteen) about the field. This required an immense amount of work. I tell everyone that I did this to become rich and famous. (My children always told me to skip the fame!) But as it turns out, all I got was the fame. However, even though I didn't make the money I had hoped for, it has still been very rewarding. Fans as far away as Australia have asked me to sign their copies of my books.

"This career has many other rewards. Uppermost is the accomplishment of developing a theory and finding supporting data. (After all, projects are funded grants for which you must show results by a certain date in order to be funded for the next project.) On the downside, the worst part of the job is when you write a paper and it gets rejected by your peers (and you think they're wrong, and in fact you know they're wrong). However, the real issue for me is that we've done some pioneering work for people that has been fruitful and rewarding.

"Here's an example. A while back we developed a way of looking at cancer in mice, and a colleague working on cancer research sent me a letter commending me on the work. The fact that somebody would think enough of our work to take what we've done and build on it is very rewarding.

"Another accomplishment relates to transplant patients. Some of the drugs used to treat these patients are very expensive, and we were able to devise a way of cutting the cost of those drugs from about $6,000 a year to about $1,200. This means that Third World countries can actually afford the drugs for their transplant patients. That's quite an accomplishment.

"To be successful in this career, it helps to have an understanding partner as I did. And since it is so important to be able to interact with people, exchange ideas, and get them to help with particular areas of your project, you must have the ability to get along with all kinds of people. You have to be aware of what issues others have and be able to accommodate them so they'll accommodate you in return. I have found that this is the proper approach to a successful collaboration. It's not unlike working with others on a book or any other project in which a number of people need to extend themselves in order to fulfill a common goal."

Meet Dennis J. Ernst

Dennis J. Ernst is currently employed by the University of Louisville Hospital in Louisville, Kentucky. He is a medical technologist, certified by the American Society of Clinical Pathologists since 1978.

"How I got started may be broken down into two parts—what attracted me to a career in the health sciences and what attracted me to a career as a medical technologist. The answers are completely different and say as much about the educational process as they do my impatience with it.

"My mother was a registered nurse whose feelings for caring for the sick inspired me back to my earliest recollection. Because of her dedication and the satisfaction she found in her work, I came to know that caring for the sick was a noble and rewarding thing. I saw her as someone who had been blessed by fate to see and know the inner workings of the human body and for me to be so blessed when I came of age was an intriguing prospect. In high school, the sciences enhanced my interest in health care so much that upon graduation I enrolled in the premed program at Albion College.

"My hopes were crushed the first week. My faculty advisor called me into his office two days after I had taken the science placement exams and said that my scores did not suggest that I was likely to succeed in the rigorous premed program. Further, he said that I was poorly prepared to major in any science curriculum whatsoever. I was stunned. If I couldn't major in the sciences, I didn't want to be on this or any other campus. Nothing else interested me. Too ignorant to take his advice and too stubborn to pursue another major, I defied his wisdom and vowed to prove him and the placement tests wrong. By the time I was a junior, I had proved them only half wrong. I was majoring in biology but pulling down only mediocre grades—far below what I needed to be considered for medical school. Though the sciences continued to intrigue me, my grade point average had eliminated not only medical school, but most other high-profile careers as well. By now the struggle had been long and hard, and I was wearing thin on persistence. I had experienced enough of education but still needed to emerge with a face-saving career of some security. The allied health fields presented many offerings but most required more postgraduate study than I had the will to endure. Then my advisor recommended medical technology, the study of blood and disease. It was perfect! I could get that inside peek at the inner workings of the human body that I still craved and with only one year of postgraduate study. I applied for internships and was accepted.

"Medical technology involves the laboratory testing of body fluids and tissues for disease. This broad category consists of many subcategories. Through the years, I have worked them all in varying degrees but am currently engaged as a clinical microbiologist in a university hospital. I test blood, tissues, and body fluids for microorganisms that cause infection. I identify the microorganisms and suggest appropriate antibiotics to fight them. My work also includes immunology, the study for the presence of disease-fighting antibodies.

"I work four eight-hour days a week, enough to be considered a full-time employee. On a typical day, I begin by retrieving and collating data. This information is printed by an automated instrument that works throughout the night to identify microorganisms by species. This is obtained from patient cultures isolated the previous day. After identification, we determine the best antibiotic therapy against the particular organism. I enter the collated information into the hospital computer system and phone any life-threatening results to the appropriate physician for immediate treatment. Once reported, I set up newly isolated organisms for the same automated, overnight testing. Also, I am responsible for the maintenance of my automated equipment and for quality control processes that assure my analytical systems are functioning properly.

"The work has obvious risks, since I can become infected by the very organisms that are infecting the patients whom I hope to help heal. However, with the proper and consistent use of personal protective devices such as gloves, gowns, and face shields (as well as implementing safe working habits), the risk is minimal. The work can be quite hectic when the hospital has many patients, but there are times when the patient population is low and the work is light. Often, there is not enough time in the day to complete all of my responsibilities. Since overtime is not allowed in our laboratory, any time spent working more than the hours scheduled must be offset by working proportionally less another day.

"Nearly all of my coworkers have either associate's or bachelor's degrees and all are certified laboratory professionals in one capacity or another. The laboratory assistants who prepare the specimens for bacterial isolation and perform a multitude of nontechnical tasks are high school graduates who have received on-the-job training. The level of cooperation among us is high, as is our goal-oriented momentum. Rarely does a day pass when someone doesn't ask me if I need any help. This is the most satisfying aspect of my work.

"Anyone interested in a career in the allied health sciences should consider medical technology for the insights it offers into the inner workings of the human body. Here one finds the constant discovery of the body's beauty and complexity that I hungered for as the young, observant son of a nurse. The intrigue has never ceased. Applications of the skills learned in training are many and varied, rendering the possibility of job burnout in this career remote. However, because of the sweeping application of managed care strategies in health care today, medical technology as a career has changed from one of promised permanence to one that is, at best, a stepping-stone to a more secure and respected calling."

Research Careers in the Physical Sciences

Chemists

Chemists search for and put to practical use new knowledge about chemicals. Although chemicals are often thought of as artificial or toxic substances, all physical things, whether naturally occurring or of human design, are composed of chemicals. Chemists have developed a tremendous variety of new and improved synthetic fibers, paints, adhesives, drugs, cosmetics, electronic components, lubricants, and thousands of other products. They also develop processes that save energy and reduce pollution, such as improved oil refining and petrochemical processing methods. Research on the chemistry of living things spurs advances in medicine, agriculture, food processing, and other areas.

In basic research, chemists investigate the properties, composition, and structure of matter and the laws that govern the combination of elements and reactions of substances. In applied research and development, they create new products and processes or improve existing ones, often using knowledge gained from basic research. For example, synthetic rubber and plastics resulted from research on small molecules uniting to form large ones (polymerization).

Chemists often specialize in a subfield. Analytical chemists determine the structure, composition, and nature of substances and develop analytical techniques. They also identify the presence and concentration of chemical pollutants in air, water, and soil. Organic chemists study the chemistry of the vast number of carbon compounds. Many commercial products, such as drugs, plastics, and fertilizers, have been developed by organic chemists. Inorganic chemists study compounds consisting mainly of

elements other than carbon, such as those in electronic components. Physical chemists study the physical characteristics of
atoms and molecules and investigate how chemical reactions
work. Their research may result in new and better energy
sources.

Physicists and Astronomers

Physicists explore and identify basic principles governing the
structure and behavior of matter, the generation and transfer of
energy, and the interaction of matter and energy. Some physicists
use these principles in theoretical areas, such as the nature of
time and the origin of the universe; others apply their physics
knowledge to practical areas, such as the development of
advanced materials, electronic and optical devices, and medical
equipment.

Physicists design and perform experiments with lasers,
cyclotrons, telescopes, mass spectrometers, and other equipment.
Based on observations and analysis, they attempt to discover the
laws that describe the forces of nature, such as gravity, electromagnetism, and nuclear interactions. They also find ways to
apply physical laws and theories to problems in nuclear energy,
electronics, optics, materials, communications, aerospace technology, navigation equipment, and medical instrumentation.

Most physicists work in research and development. Some do
basic research to increase scientific knowledge. Physicists who
conduct applied research build upon the discoveries made
through basic research and work to develop new devices, products, and processes. For instance, basic research in solid-state
physics led to the development of transistors and then to the
integrated circuits used in computers.

Physicists also design research equipment. This equipment
often has additional unanticipated uses. For example, lasers are
used in surgery; microwave devices are used for ovens; and measuring instruments can analyze blood or the chemical content of

foods. A small number work in inspection, testing, quality control, and other production-related jobs in industry.

Much physics research is done in small or medium-size laboratories. However, experiments in plasma, nuclear, and high energy and some other areas of physics require extremely large, expensive equipment such as particle accelerators. Physicists in these subfields often work in large teams. Although physics research may require extensive experimentation in laboratories, research physicists still spend time in offices planning, recording, analyzing, and reporting on research.

Physicists generally specialize in one of many subfields—elementary particle physics; nuclear physics; atomic and molecular physics; physics of condensed matter (solid-state physics); optics; acoustics; plasma physics; or the physics of fluids. Some specialize in a subdivision of one of these subfields; for example, within condensed matter physics, specialties include superconductivity, crystallography, and semiconductors. However, all physics subfields involve the same fundamental principles, so specialties may overlap, and physicists may switch from one subfield to another. Also, growing numbers of physicists work in combined fields such as biophysics, chemical physics, and geophysics.

Astronomy is sometimes considered a subfield of physics. Astronomers use the principles of physics and mathematics to learn about the fundamental nature of the universe, including the sun, moon, planets, stars, and galaxies. They also apply their knowledge to problems in navigation and space flight.

Almost all astronomers do research. They analyze large quantities of data gathered by observatories and satellites and write scientific papers or reports on their findings. Most astronomers spend only a few weeks each year making observations with optical telescopes, radio telescopes, and other instruments. Contrary to the popular image, astronomers almost never make observations by looking directly through a telescope because enhanced photographic and electronic detecting equipment can see more than the human eye.

Geologists and Geophysicists

Geologists and geophysicists, also known as geological scientists or geoscientists, study the physical aspects and history of the Earth. They identify and examine rocks, study information collected by remote sensing instruments in satellites, conduct geological surveys, construct maps, and use instruments to measure the Earth's gravity and magnetic field. They also analyze information collected through seismic studies, which involves bouncing energy waves off buried rock layers. Many geologists and geophysicists search for oil, natural gas, minerals, and groundwater.

Other geological scientists play an important role in preserving and cleaning up the environment. Their activities include designing and monitoring waste disposal sites, preserving water supplies, and reclaiming contaminated land and water to comply with federal environmental regulations. They also help locate safe sites for hazardous waste facilities and landfills.

Geologists and geophysicists examine chemical and physical properties of specimens in laboratories. They study fossil remains of animal and plant life or experiment with the flow of water and oil through rocks. Some geoscientists use two- or three-dimensional computer modeling to portray water layers and the flow of water or other fluids through rock cracks and porous materials. They use a variety of sophisticated laboratory instruments, including x-ray diffractometers to determine the crystal structure of minerals and petrographic microscopes to study rock and sediment samples. Geoscientists also use seismographs, instruments that measure energy waves resulting from movements in the Earth's crust, to determine the locations and intensities of earthquakes.

Geoscientists working in the oil and gas industry sometimes process and interpret the maps produced by remote sensing satellites to help identify potential new oil or gas deposits. Seismic technology is also an important exploration tool. Seismic waves are used to develop three-dimensional computer models of underground or underwater rock formations.

Geologists and geophysicists also apply geological knowledge to engineering problems in constructing large buildings, dams, tunnels, and highways. Some administer and manage research and exploration programs.

Geology and geophysics are closely related fields, but there are major differences. Geologists study the composition, structure, and history of the Earth's crust. They try to find out how rocks were formed and what has happened to them since their formation. Geophysicists use the principles of physics and mathematics to study not only the Earth's surface but its internal composition, ground and surface waters, atmosphere, and oceans, as well as its magnetic, electrical, and gravitational forces. Both, however, commonly apply their skills to the search for natural resources and to solve environmental problems.

There are numerous subdisciplines or specialties that fall under the two major disciplines of geology and geophysics, which further differentiate the kind of work geoscientists do. For example, petroleum geologists explore for oil and gas deposits by studying and mapping the subsurface of the ocean or land. They use sophisticated geophysical instrumentation, well log data, and computers to collect information. Mineralogists analyze and classify minerals and precious stones according to composition and structure. Paleontologists study fossils found in geological formations to trace the evolution of plant and animal life and the geologic history of the Earth. Stratigraphers help to locate minerals by studying the distribution and arrangement of sedimentary rock layers and by examining the fossil and mineral content of such layers. Those who study marine geology are usually called oceanographers or marine geologists. They study and map the ocean floor and collect information using remote sensing devices aboard surface ships or underwater research crafts.

Geophysicists may specialize in areas such as geodesy, seismology, or marine geophysics, also known as physical oceanography. Geodesists study the Earth's size, shape, gravitational field, tides, polar motion, and rotation. Seismologists interpret data from seismographs and other geophysical instruments to detect earthquakes and locate earthquake-related faults. Physical oceanographers study the physical aspects of oceans, such as currents and the interaction of sea surface and atmosphere.

Hydrology is a discipline closely related to geology and geophysics. Hydrologists study the distribution, circulation, and physical properties of underground and surface waters. They study the form and intensity of precipitation, its rate of infiltration into the soil, movement through the earth, and its return to the ocean and atmosphere. The work they do is particularly important in environmental preservation and remediation.

Meteorologists

Meteorology is the study of the atmosphere, the air that covers the Earth. Meteorologists study the atmosphere's physical characteristics, motions, and processes and the way it affects the rest of our environment. The best-known application of this knowledge is in forecasting the weather. However, weather information and meteorological research also are applied in air-pollution control, agriculture, air and sea transportation, defense, and the study of trends in the Earth's climate, such as global warming or ozone depletion.

Meteorologists who forecast the weather, known professionally as operational meteorologists, are the largest group of specialists. They study information on air pressure, temperature, humidity, and wind velocity, and they apply physical and mathematical relationships to make short- and long-range weather forecasts. Their data comes from weather satellites, weather radar, and remote sensors and observers in many parts of the world. Meteorologists use sophisticated computer models of the world's atmosphere to make long-term, short-term, and local-area forecasts. These forecasts inform not only the general public but also those who need accurate weather information for both economic and safety reasons, as in the shipping, aviation, agriculture, fishing, and utilities industries.

The use of weather balloons, launched several times a day, to measure wind, temperature, and humidity in the upper atmosphere is supplemented by far more sophisticated weather equipment that transmits data as frequently as every few minutes. Doppler radar, for example, can detect rotational patterns in violent storm systems, allowing forecasters to better predict thunderstorms, tornadoes, and flash floods, as well as their direction and intensity.

Physical meteorologists study the atmosphere's chemical and physical properties; the transmission of light, sound, and radio waves; and the transfer of energy in the atmosphere. They also study factors affecting formation of clouds, rain, snow, and other weather phenomena, such as severe storms. Climatologists collect, analyze, and interpret past records of wind, rainfall, sunshine, and temperature in specific areas or regions. Their studies are used to design buildings, plan heating and cooling systems, aid in effective land use, and increase agricultural production. Other research meteorologists examine the most effective ways to control or diminish air pollution or improve weather forecasting using mathematical models.

Training for Research Careers in the Physical Sciences

Training for Chemists

A bachelor's degree in chemistry or a related discipline is usually the minimum education necessary to work as a chemist. However, many, if not most, research jobs require a Ph.D. degree. Many colleges and universities offer a bachelor's degree program in chemistry, more than six hundred of which are approved by the American Chemical Society. Several hundred colleges and universities also offer advanced degree programs in chemistry.

Students planning careers as chemists should enjoy studying science and mathematics and should like working with their hands building scientific apparatus and performing experiments. Perseverance, curiosity, and the ability to concentrate on detail and to work independently are essential. In addition to required courses in analytical, inorganic, organic, and physical chemistry, undergraduate chemistry majors usually study biological sciences, mathematics, and physics. Computer courses are invaluable, as employers increasingly prefer job applicants who are computer literate and who can apply computer skills to modeling and simulation tasks. Laboratory instruments are also computerized, and the ability to operate and understand equipment is essential.

Because research and development chemists are increasingly expected to work on interdisciplinary teams, some understanding of other disciplines, including business and marketing or economics, is desirable, along with leadership ability and good oral and written communication skills. Experience in academic laboratories or through internships or co-op programs in industry also is useful. Some employers of research chemists, particularly in the pharmaceutical industry, prefer to hire individuals with several years of postdoctoral experience.

Although graduate students typically specialize in a subfield of chemistry, such as analytical chemistry or polymer chemistry, students usually need not specialize at the undergraduate level. In fact, undergraduates who are broadly trained have more flexibility when job hunting or changing jobs than if they narrowly define their interests. Most employers provide new bachelor's degree chemists with additional training or education.

In government or industry, beginning chemists with bachelor's degrees work in technical sales or services and quality control, or they assist senior chemists in research and development laboratories. Some may work in research positions, analyzing and testing products, but these may be positions as technicians, with limited upward mobility. Many employers prefer chemists with a Ph.D. to work in basic and applied research. A Ph.D. is also generally preferred for advancement to many administrative positions. Chemists who work in professional research positions often eventually move into management.

Many people with a bachelor's degree in chemistry enter other occupations in which a chemistry background is helpful, such as technical writing or chemical marketing. Some enter medical, dental, veterinary, or other health profession schools.

Training for Physicists and Astronomers

A doctoral degree is the usual educational requirement for physicists and astronomers, because most jobs are in research and development. Many physics and astronomy Ph.D. holders ultimately take jobs teaching at the college or university level. Additional experience and training in a postdoctoral research assignment, although not required, is helpful in preparing physicists and astronomers for permanent research positions.

Those having bachelor's or master's degrees in physics are rarely qualified to fill positions as physicists. They are, however, usually qualified to work in an engineering-related area, in other scientific fields, as technicians, or they may assist in setting up laboratories. Some may qualify for applied research jobs in private industry or for nonresearch positions in the federal government. A master's degree often suffices for teaching jobs in two-year colleges. Astronomy bachelor's degree holders often enter fields unrelated to astronomy, but they are also qualified to work in planetariums running science shows or to assist astronomers doing research.

Hundreds of colleges and universities offer bachelor's degrees in physics. The undergraduate program provides a broad background in the natural sciences and mathematics. Typical physics courses include mechanics, electromagnetism, optics, thermodynamics, atomic physics, and quantum mechanics.

About 180 colleges and universities have physics departments that offer Ph.D. degrees in physics. Graduate students usually concentrate in a subfield of physics, such as elementary particles or condensed matter. Many begin studying for a doctorate immediately after earning a bachelor's degree.

About forty universities offer Ph.D. degrees in astronomy, either through an astronomy department, a physics department, or a combined physics/astronomy department. Applicants to astronomy doctoral programs face keen competition for available slots. Those planning a career in astronomy should have a very strong physics background. In fact, an undergraduate degree in physics is excellent preparation, followed by a Ph.D. in astronomy.

Mathematical ability, computer skills, an inquisitive mind, imagination, and the ability to work independently are important traits for anyone planning a career in physics or astronomy. Prospective physicists who hope to work in industrial laboratories applying physics knowledge to practical problems should broaden their educational backgrounds to include courses outside of physics, such as economics, computer technology, and current affairs. Good oral and written communication skills are also important because many physicists work as part of a team or have contact with persons with nonphysics backgrounds, such as clients or customers.

Most Ph.D. physics and astronomy graduates begin their careers conducting research in postdoctoral positions, where they may work with experienced physicists as they continue to learn about their specialties and develop ideas and results to be used in later work. The initial work may be routine and under the close supervision of senior scientists. After some experience, they perform more complex tasks and work more independently. Physicists who develop new products or processes sometimes form their own companies or join new firms to exploit their own ideas.

Training for Geologists and Geophysicists

A bachelor's degree in geology or geophysics is adequate for entry into some lower-level geology jobs, but better jobs with good advancement potential usually require at least a master's degree in geology or geophysics. Persons with strong backgrounds in physics, chemistry, mathematics, or computer science also may qualify for some geophysics or geology jobs. A Ph.D. degree is required for most research positions in colleges and universities and is also important for work in federal agencies and some state geological surveys that involve basic research.

Hundreds of colleges and universities offer a bachelor's degree program in geology, geophysics, oceanography, or other geoscience. Other programs offering related training for beginning geological scientists include geophysical technology, geophysical engineering, geophysical prospecting, engineering geology, petroleum geology, hydrology, and geochemistry. In addition, several hundred more universities award advanced degrees in geology or geophysics.

Geologists and geophysicists need to be able to work as part of a team. Computer modeling, data processing, and effective oral and written communication skills are important, as well as the ability to think independently and creatively. Those involved in fieldwork must have physical stamina.

Traditional geoscience courses emphasizing classical geologic methods and topics (such as mineralology, paleontology, stratigraphy, and structural geology) are important for all geoscientists. However, those students interested in working in the environmental or regulatory fields should take courses in hydrology, hazardous waste management, environmental legislation, chemistry, mechanics, and geologic logging. Also, some employers seek applicants with field experience, so a summer internship or employment in an environmentally related area may be beneficial to prospective geoscientists.

Geologists and geophysicists often begin their careers in field exploration or as research assistants in laboratories. They are given more difficult assignments as they gain experience. Eventually they may be promoted to project leaders, program managers, or other management or research positions.

Training for Meteorologists

A bachelor's degree with a major in meteorology or a closely related field with course work in meteorology is the usual minimum requirement for a beginning job as a meteorologist.

The preferred educational requirement for entry-level meteorologists in the federal government is a bachelor's degree (not necessarily in meteorology) with at least twenty semester hours of meteorology courses, including six hours in weather analysis and forecasting and six hours in dynamic meteorology. In addition to meteorology course work, differential and integral calculus and six hours of college physics are required. These requirements have recently been upgraded to include course work in computer science and additional course work appropriate for a physical science major, such as statistics, chemistry, physical oceanography, or physical climatology. Sometimes, a combination of experience and education may be substituted for a degree.

Although positions in operational meteorology are available for applicants with only bachelor's degrees, graduate degrees enhance advancement potential. A master's degree is usually necessary for conducting research and development, and a Ph.D. may be required for some research positions. Students who plan a career in research and development need not necessarily major in meteorology as undergraduates. In fact, a bachelor's degree in mathematics, physics, or engineering is excellent preparation for graduate study in meteorology.

The federal government's National Weather Service is the largest employer of civilian meteorologists. Because meteorology is a small field, relatively few colleges and universities offer degrees in meteorology or atmospheric science, although many departments of physics, Earth science, geography, and geophysics offer atmospheric science and related courses. Prospective students should make certain that courses required by the National Weather Service and other employers are offered at the colleges they are considering. Computer science courses, additional meteorology courses, and a strong background in mathematics and physics are important to prospective employers. Many programs combine the study of meteorology with another field, such as agriculture, engineering, or physics. For example, hydrometeorology is the blending of hydrology (the science of the Earth's water) and meteorology and is the field concerned with the effect of precipitation on the hydrologic cycle and the environment.

Beginning meteorologists often do routine data collection, computation, or analysis and some basic forecasting. Entry-level meteorologists in the federal government are usually placed in intern positions for training and experience. Experienced meteorologists may advance to various supervisory or administrative jobs or may handle more complex forecasting jobs. Increasing numbers of meteorologists establish their own weather consulting services.

Earnings for Research Careers in the Physical Sciences

Chemists

According to a 1997 survey by the American Chemical Society, the median salary for members with bachelor's degrees was $49,400; with master's degrees, $56,200; and with doctorates, $71,000. In 1997, chemists in nonsupervisory, supervisory, and managerial positions in the federal government earned average salaries of $60,000.

Physicists and Astronomers

The American Institute of Physics reported a median salary of $65,000 in 1997 for its members with doctorates. Those with master's degrees earned about $55,000, and those with bachelor's degrees, $50,000.

According to a 1997 National Association of Colleges and Employers survey, the average starting salary offered to physics doctoral degree candidates was $34,700.

Average annual earnings for physicists in nonsupervisory, supervisory, and managerial positions in the federal government in 1997 were about $71,800 and for astronomy and space scientists, $77,400.

Geologists and Geophysicists

Surveys by the National Association of Colleges and Employers indicate that graduates with bachelor's degrees in geology and the geological sciences received an average starting offer of about $30,900 a year in 1997. However, starting salaries can vary widely, depending on the employing industry. For example, according to a 1996 American Association of Petroleum Geologists survey, the average salary in the oil and gas industry for geoscientists with less than two years of experience was about $48,400. Although petroleum, mineral, and mining industries offer higher salaries, the competition in these areas is normally intense, and the job security is less than in other areas.

In 1997, the federal government's average salary for geologists in managerial, supervisory, and nonsupervisory positions was $59,700; for geophysicists, $67,100; for hydrologists, $54,800; and for oceanographers, $62,700.

Meteorologists

The average salary for meteorologists in nonsupervisory, supervisory, and managerial positions employed by the federal government was about $57,000 in 1997.

Meet Some Physical Sciences Researchers

Meet Ken Rubin, Ph.D.

Dr. Rubin serves as an assistant professor on the staff of the University of Hawaii in the department of geology and geophysics, School of Ocean and Earth Science and Technology (SOEST).

"I earned my B.A. from the University of California-San Diego in chemistry in 1984. Following this, I pursued my graduate training at the University of California-San Diego, Scripps Institute of Oceanography and received my M.S. in 1985 and my Ph.D. in 1991. I came to the University of Hawaii in February of 1992 as an assistant researcher and became an assistant professor in January of 1995.

"Essentially, I was hired at the University of Hawaii right out of graduate school (although I spent about nine months doing postdoctorate work at Scripps Institution of Oceanography before actually starting my job at UH). I was hired in a competitive search for a postdoctorate position known as the SOEST Young Investigator. This position is better than a simple postdoctorate in that it is actually a research faculty position (at the assistant level) that allows one to write grant proposals to federal funding agencies and to work independent of a supervisor. SOEST offers one or two of these positions a year, with applicants being chosen from a variety of disciplines (Earth sciences, oceanography, marine biology, atmospheric sciences, ocean engineering). Other universities offer these sorts of 'institutional' postdoctorate positions with varying levels of support and duration.

"Once at the University of Hawaii, I entered into an agreement with our school's dean and other faculty to set up a state-of-the-art thermal ionization mass spectrometry facility for analyzing radioactive isotopes. This was a serious commitment for all involved, because the time frame for getting a lab of this sort funded and up and running is three to five years, longer than the two-year position I was given. However, I was given verbal agreement that, pending significant productivity on my part, my assistant researcher position could be extended beyond the original two-year period.

"At the time (1992), there were only two other facilities of this type in the country (outside of restricted-access national laboratories). Now there are probably five or so. Setting up the lab required getting federal support for the purchase of a $750,000 mass spectrometer. I funded it with 25 percent each from the National Science Foundation Earth Sciences and Ocean Sciences Divisions and 50 percent from SOEST.

"After successfully getting the instrument funded and starting to get the laboratory set up, I was offered an assistant professor position at the University of Miami's Rosenstiel School of Marine and Atmospheric Sciences (RSMAS). At the time (spring 1994), the state of Hawaii was just entering an economic downturn, and I felt it was necessary to encourage the university into making our relationship more 'formal' by getting a solid offer from another institution. I would have been willing to move to another locale but preferred to continue here at UH. Following this, an assistant professor position was approved by SOEST and the UH, a national search was conducted, and I was chosen for the position. So, here I am.

"I started undergraduate school wanting to be an M.D. But, during my freshman year, I became really turned on to chemistry with environmental applications. Simultaneously, I fell in love with the academician's career and lifestyle. I immediately changed my career aspirations to becoming a professor at a research university. I have nothing against private sector or government jobs, and know I could find some level of fulfillment in pursuits there. However, it was clear to me then and still is today that the level of intellectual freedom that the university system in America affords makes this sort of job highly rewarding.

"I work seven days a week, between eight and twelve hours a day. Part of this may be because I am not yet tenured, and part of it is because my particular brand of research requires lengthy and exacting analytical procedures in a clean-room environment that makes progress slow unless you put in long hours. But part of why I work so much is simply because I enjoy it and have taken on other nonresearch and nonteaching duties as extras.

"I teach one or two upper-division and/or graduate-level class-room courses per semester and presently am advising three graduate students (two doctoral, one master's). I do my lab research in one- to two-month chunks where I may spend all my non-classroom time in the lab or in the field (both on oceangoing research vessels and on land) or in my office reducing data and interpreting results.

"Some of my fieldwork, which includes research on active volcanoes on land and on the sea floor, is dangerous, and almost all of my lab work involves toxic chemicals and radioactive substances. This work isn't for everyone, but I find it rewarding because of the day-to-day challenges. The part that makes it unique, and the difficult thing to pass on to students, is the application of high-precision measurements requiring exacting care and uncompromising standards to natural phenomena. Although the lab and fieldwork are both necessary aspects of the research we do, the two environments are very different and require different mind-sets.

"In addition to these things, I have also worked to get our school (SOEST) and its departments, students, and faculty on-line to the Internet. I developed and oversee numerous Web sites at our school, including interactive sites providing answers to the public to questions about science, and resource sites dedicated to educating lay people and researchers about active processes at volcanoes and the latest research going on at the University of

Hawaii. I use the Internet in my courses and love what it offers. Once a person relates to and accepts the way in which people make computers process and make information available, their mind is freed to cross the boundaries between the abstract and the physical. Computers are a wonderful and indispensable teaching tool.

"There are, of course, many trade-offs with this sort of job. To enjoy the academic and intellectual freedom, friendly atmosphere, youthful environment, and flexible hours, one must be very disciplined. This can make it difficult, as you must evaluate yourself and your progress frequently and cannot rely on infrequent or nonexistent direction from a superior. You must sense the expectations of your peers and then work to satisfy them while not sacrificing your own goals and desires. You must be self-motivated and take a very long-range perspective on success in the attainment of work-related goals.

"Additionally, today's academic scientist must deal with lack of funds at all levels. The golden age of scientific research died out in the 1980s (if not earlier). I watch my older colleagues struggling to adapt to this new environment, but since I never knew the days of seemingly unlimited research funds, I don't get as depressed as they at the difficulty of getting research funded today.

"Jobs are very difficult to obtain, so always work hard at everything you do. Not only are top-notch resumes required to land one of these jobs, but hard work will be required to keep it. A university professor's life may appear to be genteel and rewarding and filled with healthy doses of wisdom and cups of cappuccino at the local coffeehouse, but it is actually rigorous on many levels."

Meet Glen D. Lawrence, Ph.D.

Dr. Lawrence has been affiliated with Long Island University since 1985. He received his B.S. in chemistry from Pratt Institute in Brooklyn, New York; his M.A. in chemistry from SUNY at Plattsburgh, New York; and his Ph.D. in biochemistry from Utah State University in Logan, Utah. He served as a science advisor for the U.S. Food and Drug Administration New York Regional Laboratory from 1988 to 1992, advising analytical chemists in research projects related to drug chemistry.

"I grew up on a farm in rural New York and always had a curiosity about how living organisms functioned. However, I had few role models who were scientists in my community (in fact, none that I can think of) and a very poor guidance counselor in high school, so I had little idea what direction I wanted to take after completing high school. I did well in science and math in school and decided to pursue a career in chemistry. As I began studies in chemistry, I realized that my fascination was with biochemistry, so I enrolled in a master's degree program in a chemistry department, with a biochemist as my research advisor. This mentor was recommended by one of my high school friends who had gone to that college as an undergraduate. After completing my master's degree, I had a taste of the academic research life and knew that I wanted to pursue that option. I applied to graduate school in Utah at the suggestion of one of the professors where I had received my M.A. degree and went there to study for the Ph.D. in biochemistry.

"After completing my Ph.D., I applied for a research fellowship to study model systems for photosynthesis, with the support of an NSF Energy-Related Postdoctoral Fellowship. I was always conservation minded and wanted to do studies on the development of materials that could be used to convert solar energy into useful chemical energy. This specific project was aimed at developing materials that would utilize light to catalyze the splitting of water into hydrogen and oxygen, which could later be used as fuels. After studying this problem for a year in West Germany (1976–77), I came to the realization that it was a difficult task to accomplish (mimicking nature generally is not easy to accomplish in the chemistry laboratory). I spent several years pursuing research at several different laboratories (University of California-Riverside, Mt. Sinai, and Columbia University) and found these research opportunities to be extremely valuable to me in broadening my knowledge of science in general and biochemistry, pharmacology, physiology, and toxicology in particular.

"I started at LIU in 1985, while a research fellow at the Institute of Human Nutrition at Columbia University," says Dr. Lawrence. "Funding for my research project was ending, and, although I was coauthor of another funded research grant, there had been an administrative error that made me ineligible for financial support from that grant for another year. I therefore actively pursued a teaching position, which was my ultimate career goal. Although I was planning to hold out for a faculty position at a research institution, the master's degree program at the LIU Brooklyn campus provided ample opportunity for research, along with interesting possibilities for teaching advanced courses in special areas, such as neurochemistry and advanced analytical techniques for biomedical analysis.

"As a professor of chemistry in a department that offers a master's degree, I am responsible for teaching about nine hours of courses per week during a typical academic year. I teach a wide range of college courses, including any of the following during any given academic year: introductory chemistry for nonscience (liberal arts) majors (three hours of lecture and two hours of lab per week); chemistry for the health sciences (three hours lecture and two and one-half hours of lab per week); biochemistry to chemistry and molecular biology majors (three hours of lecture and three hours of lab per week); and graduate courses in analytical chemistry, biochemistry, and neurochemistry (each three hours of lecture per week). Occasionally I offer an elective course for honors students (the one I offered last fall was entitled 'Drugs in Our Culture.' Of course, I don't teach all of these courses in any given year, since it adds up to much more than nine hours per week.

"In addition to teaching, I usually advise undergraduate and graduate students in research projects This past spring I had two undergraduate students working with me on two separate projects. One student was analyzing naltrexone, a morphine-like drug that was being used in a study with hypertensive, stroke-prone rats. The animal study was performed by a colleague in the School of Pharmacy at LIU. Our job in the chemistry department was to measure the drug taken from blood samples from these rats. The amount of blood you can get from a rat is very small (about 0.5 ml), so our procedure had to be suitable for measuring tiny amounts of this potent drug in very small amounts. We were successful in developing the method, after much time was spent trying to fine-tune the analytical instrument needed to make these measurements.

"The other project was a study of the effect of combining vitamin C with aspartame (the artificial sweetener known as Nutrasweet) and measuring the products that result from combining these two food additives. We were interested to see if there are any products that could be potentially harmful to our health. Again, this required the analysis of trace amounts of substances in a complex mixture of things.

"The lab that my students and I work in is very small and cramped (only about seven feet by fifteen feet, including a sink, a hood, a cabinet for glassware, and bench space for pH meter, stirrers for mixing solutions, and some small analytical instruments). Some of the instruments we use are in another large room that contains only special analytical instruments.

"Although the work is not dangerous, we must take the proper precautions when performing some experiments. The materials we work with are usually not explosive in nature, nor are most of them very toxic. However, we must be aware of the things that are toxic or explosive and handle them in a way that is not going to result in a perilous situation.

"Some years ago, I worked as a science advisor for the Food and Drug Administration. That job required that I go to the

FDA labs one day a week and discuss research projects with the analytical chemists there. Their jobs primarily involved analyzing the drugs being sold by pharmaceutical companies. The FDA must use well-established methods for drug analysis that have undergone extensive testing in both the FDA labs as well as the pharmaceutical manufacturers' labs. Some of these methods rely on procedures that may be many years old, but newer methods could save much time without sacrificing accuracy. However, any new method must be tested before it can become an established method in their protocol. My job was to work with the chemists there to try to streamline the methods used to accomplish efficient and accurate drug analysis. One example was a method for analyzing the drugs in nerve gas antidotes for the U.S. Department of Defense. When the Persian Gulf war broke out, nerve gas antidotes had to be removed from storage and tested quickly to make sure they were suitable for use, since much of the stockpile had passed the expiration date. The existing method required approximately forty-five minutes per sample for testing. I tried a different method that I thought would work, and it resulted in decreasing the analysis time to about ten minutes. This isn't a great deal for a few samples, but when there were hundreds of lots of drug samples that had to be analyzed, this decrease in time would mean a savings of weeks or months in analysis time. However, the new method had to be thoroughly tested before it could be implemented. It turned out to be very suitable, not only for military samples but for a wide variety of dosage forms, including eye drops and some other medications.

"As a professor, I also serve on various committees around the campus. Though these committees vary from year to year, all take up a substantial amount of time. The committee work may include the evaluation of junior faculty members for promotion and tenure, discussion of new courses and curricula that are being proposed for the university, review of existing courses and programs and the regular reevaluation of the campus for accreditation, or attention to the day-to-day running of the university.

"In addition, I am often asked to review a master's degree candidate's thesis to determine whether the student meets our approval to obtain a degree. If I am the student's advisor, it may require sitting down with the candidate, advising him or her how to go about writing a master's thesis (as well as reading the thesis over many times to make all the necessary corrections before it is submitted to the student's committee). This all occurs after guiding the student through a research project that usually lasts about a year. Although the student doesn't work on the project full-time, he or she may put in ten to twenty hours per week doing the research in the lab. This requires developing methods for analyzing certain chemicals that may be of interest to us, collecting a wealth of data to support a hypothesis, analyzing the data to see if it supports the hypothesis, then finally deciding how to present the data so it will be understandable to others who may be interested.

"Whether in the classroom or the laboratory, teaching can be very exciting. Other times it can be extremely frustrating. Sometimes students show a genuine interest in the material; other times I get a whole classroom of students who just don't want to be there (but it is a requirement for them to graduate). Many come into the class dreading it initially but find after a while that we are covering things that can be quite interesting, such as the greenhouse effect, global warming, air and water pollution, destruction of the ozone layer, and guidelines about how to keep your body healthy. By the time the students get finished, some of them realize that it was a worthwhile college experience.

"Probably the most rewarding aspect of my job is realized when a student decides to do a special project, either in the form of research in the lab or a library research project, and that student begins to comprehend the complexities of science, especially the life sciences. If I feel that I could instill in another individual the desire to pursue a career in science or just to understand more about how the world works on the molecular level, then I feel I have accomplished my goal. Even if only a handful of my students realize this in my lifetime, I will have passed something on to the next generation."

For More Information

Biological and Medical Sciences

For information on careers in physiology, contact:

American Physiological Society
Membership Services Department
9650 Rockville Pike
Bethesda, MD 20814

For information on careers in biotechnology, contact:

Biotechnology Industry Organization
1625 K Street NW, Suite 1100
Washington, DC 20006

For information on careers in biochemistry, contact:

American Society for Biochemistry and Molecular Biology
9650 Rockville Pike
Bethesda, MD 20814

For information on careers in botany, contact:

Business Office
Botanical Society of America
1725 Neil Avenue
Columbus, OH 43210-1293

For information on careers in microbiology, contact:

American Society for Microbiology
Office of Education and Training-Career Information
1325 Massachusetts Avenue NW
Washington, DC 20005

Information on federal job opportunities in scientific research is available from local offices of state employment services or offices of the United States Office of Personnel Management, located in major metropolitan areas.

Physical Sciences

General information on career opportunities and earnings for chemists is available from:

American Chemical Society
Department of Career Services
1155 Sixteenth Street NW
Washington, DC 20036

General information on career opportunities in physics is available from:

American Institute of Physics
Career Planning and Placement
One Physics Ellipse
College Park, MD 20740-3843

American Physical Society
Education Department
One Physics Ellipse
College Park, MD 20740-3844

For a pamphlet containing information on careers in astronomy, send your request to:

American Astronomical Society
Education Office
University of Texas
Department of Astronomy
Austin, TX 78712-1083

Information on training and career opportunities for geologists is available from:

American Geological Institute
4220 King Street
Alexandria, VA 22302-1507

Geological Society of America
P.O. Box 9140
3300 Penrose Place
Boulder, CO 80301

American Association of Petroleum Geologists
Communications Department
P.O. Box 979
Tulsa, OK 74101

Information on training and career opportunities for geophysicists is available from:

American Geophysical Union
2000 Florida Avenue NW
Washington, DC 20009

A list of curricula in colleges and universities offering programs in oceanography and related fields is available from:

Marine Technology Society
1828 L Street NW, Suite 906
Washington, DC 20036

Information on career opportunities in meteorology is available from:

American Meteorological Society
45 Beacon Street
Boston, MA 02108

National Oceanic and Atmospheric Administration
Human Resources Management Office
1315 East West Highway
Route Code OA/22
Silver Spring, MD 20910

Information on federal job opportunities in the physical sciences is available from local offices of state employment services or branches of the United States Office of Personnel Management, located in major metropolitan areas.

CHAPTER SIX

Careers in Entertainment

"Acting is the most minor of gifts. After all, Shirley Temple could do it when she was four." KATHARINE HEPBURN

Welcome to the World of Acting

Based on scripts, actors perform their roles in theaters, movies, and radio and television productions. Whether the characters they are portraying are young or old, or the part is dramatic or comedic, actors bring their characters "to life" using voices, gestures, and movements.

Though acting is often viewed as a glamorous profession, the truth is that many actors are forced to put in long and irregular hours (including rehearsals and performances) with little payment in return. In addition, only a few actors achieve recognition as stars on the stage, in motion pictures, or on television. More actors are well-known, experienced performers who frequently are cast in supporting roles. Most actors struggle to "break into" the profession and pick up parts wherever they can. Many successful actors continue to accept small roles, including commercials and product endorsements. Some actors employed by theater companies teach acting courses to the public.

Training for Actors

Successful actors recommend that those who aspire to this profession should take part in high school and college plays for the experience these activities provide. Large cities like Chicago,

New York, and Los Angeles have public high schools especially for the performing arts.

Formal dramatic training, and/or acting experience, is generally necessary, although some people enter the field without either. Training can be obtained at dramatic arts schools in New York and Los Angeles and at colleges and universities throughout the country offering bachelor's or graduate degrees in dramatic and theater arts. A master's degree in theater is considered an additional plus. Most people take college courses in liberal arts, theater, directing, play production, design, playwriting, speech and movement, acting, and dramatic literature. Many experienced actors get additional formal training to learn new skills and improve on old ones.

Desirable Qualities

Desirable personal qualities for actors include talent, determination, perseverance, persistence, social skills, a good memory, a fine speaking voice, creative ability, and training that will enable them to portray different characters. Training in singing and dancing is especially useful. Actors must have poise, stage presence, the ability to affect an audience, plus the ability to follow directions. Physical appearance is often a deciding factor in being selected for particular roles.

Actors need stamina to withstand the heat of stage or studio lights; heavy costumes; the long, irregular hours; and the adverse weather conditions that may exist "on location."

Building a Career

The best way to start building an acting career is to pursue local opportunities and then move on from there. Acting group and local and regional theater experience may help in obtaining work in New York or Los Angeles. Modeling experience may also be helpful.

Most actors list themselves with casting agencies that help them find parts. Many also take advantage of the services offered by the unions listed at the end of this chapter. Many professional actors rely on agents or managers to find work, negotiate contracts, and plan their careers. Agents generally earn a percentage of an actor's contract.

As actors' reputations grow, they work on larger productions or in more prestigious theaters. Actors also advance to lead or specialized roles. A few actors move into acting-related jobs as drama coaches or directors of stage, television, radio, or motion picture productions. Some teach drama in colleges and universities.

The length of a performer's working life depends largely on training, skill, versatility, and perseverance. Some actors continue working throughout their lives; however, many leave the occupation after a short time because they cannot find enough work to make a living.

Extra! Extra! Read All About It!

In addition to the actors with speaking parts, "extras," who have small parts with no lines to deliver, are used throughout the industry. To become a movie extra (also known as a 'background artist'), one must usually be listed by a casting agency, such as Central Casting, a no-fee agency that supplies extras to the major movie studios in Hollywood. Applicants are accepted only when the number of persons of a particular type on the list is below the foreseeable need. In recent years, only a very small proportion of the applicants have succeeded in being listed.

Acting Strategies—Finding a Job

Armed with your college degree, basic knowledge of the acting business, and some experience, you'll need to prepare a portfolio to highlight your qualifications, acting history, and special skills. This will take the form of a resume. You will also need to have photos taken by a professional photographer (one who shows you off to your best advantage). These are the essential tools of your trade. Attach your resume to the back of your picture with one staple at the upper left- and right-hand corners. Once you have your portfolio ready, you can start "making the rounds" of casting offices, ad agencies, producers' offices, and agents. Several trade newspapers contain casting information, ads for part-time jobs, information about shows, and other pertinent data about what's going on in the industry. Among these are *Back Stage* in New York and Los Angeles and *Ross Reports* in New York. There is also the weekly *Variety*. In Los Angeles, there's also *Daily Variety*, the *Hollywood Reporter*, and *Drama-Logue*. You will even be able to find out about casting calls and other opportunities on-line through the Internet.

Once you drop off your resumes and head shots, you certainly shouldn't just sit at home waiting for the phone to ring. It's wise to stay in contact—stop by and say hello. Check in by phone every week to see if any opportunities are available for you. If you are currently in a show, send prospective employers a flyer. It shows them that you are a working actor.

When you get past this initial stage and actually win an audition, here are eight audition tips you should remember:

1. Be prepared.

2. Be familiar with the piece—read it beforehand and choose the parts you'd like to try out for.

3. Go for it—don't hold back.

4. Speak loudly and clearly—project to the back of the room.

5. Take chances.

6. Try not to go first—observe others so you can pick up on what the evaluators seem to like or dislike.

7. Appear enthusiastic and confident.

8. Keep auditioning—even if you don't get parts. You are getting invaluable experience that is bound to pay off.

So, when do you get an agent? Not right away, anyway. First of all, you don't need an agent to audition for everything. There are many things you can audition for that do not require an agent—theater, nonunion films, union films. However, most commercials are cast through agencies, so you would most likely need an agent to land one of those.

While waiting to be chosen for a part, acting hopefuls often take jobs as waiters, bartenders, taxi drivers—positions that afford a flexible schedule and some money to live on.

Earnings for Actors

Minimum salaries, hours of work, and other conditions of employment are covered in collective bargaining agreements between producers of shows and unions representing workers in this field. The Actors Equity Association represents stage actors; the Screen Actors Guild (SAG) and the Screen Extras Guild cover actors in motion pictures, including television, commercials, and films; and the American Federation of Television and Radio Artists (AFTRA) represents television and radio performers. Of course, any actor may negotiate for a salary higher than the minimum.

According to limited information, the minimum weekly salary for actors in Broadway stage productions is $1,000. Those in small "off-Broadway" theaters receive minimums ranging from $380 to $650 a week, depending on the seating capacity of the theater. For shows on the road, actors receive about $100 per day more for living expenses. Actors usually work long hours during rehearsals. Once the show opens, they have more regular hours, working about thirty hours per week.

According to the Screen Actors Guild, motion picture and television actors with speaking parts earn a minimum daily rate of about $500, or $1,750 for a five-day week. Those without speaking parts—extras—earn a minimum daily rate of about $100. Actors also receive contributions to their health and pension plans and additional compensation for reruns.

Earnings from acting are low because employment is so irregular. The Screen Actors Guild also reports that the average income its members earn from acting is $1,400 a year, and 80 percent of its members earn less than $5,000 a year from acting. Therefore, many actors must supplement their incomes by holding jobs in other fields.

Some well-known actors have salary rates well above the minimums, and the salaries of the few top stars are many times the figures cited, creating a false impression that all actors are highly paid. Many actors who work more than a set number of weeks per year are covered by a union health, welfare, and pension fund, including hospitalization insurance, to which employers contribute. Under some employment conditions, Actors Equity and AFTRA members receive paid vacations and sick leave.

Meet Some Professional Actors

Meet Jennifer Aquino

Jennifer Aquino studied theater and dance at the University of California in Los Angeles and received a bachelor of arts degree in economics. As a member of the dance team, she was a UCLA cheerleader for three years. In addition to cheering for UCLA's football and basketball teams, she also entered national dance team competitions.

"I grew up in Cerritos, California, and received my first taste of acting at St. Linus elementary school in Norwalk where I played the leading role of the princess in *Beyond the Horizon*, says Aquino. "Happily, I received the Performing Arts Award while attending Whitney High School.

"Following my college graduation, I got my first break playing Eolani, the wife of Dr. Jacoby in David Lynch's television series *Twin Peaks* (a result of my very first audition). Then I got an agent and joined the Screen Actors Guild. I have been performing in various theatrical productions and am a founding member of Theatre Geo, as well as an active member of Theatre West and the East West Players Network. (Watch for me in a national commercial for Ford trucks!)

"My television credits include *Weird Science; The Paranormal Borderline; Fresh Prince of Bel Air; Santa Barbara;* and *Twin Peaks.*

"Film credits include *The Party Crashers; Prisoners of Love;* AFI's *it makes you wonder . . how a girl can keep from going under,* UCLA's, *Fleeting Vanities of Life,* USC's *Unexpected Love,* and NYU's *Free Love.*

"Theater Credits include *People Like Me* at the Playwrights Arena; *Gila River* at Japan America Theatre and at Scottsdale Center for the Arts in Arizona; *Cabaret* and *Sophisticated Barflies* at East West Players; PAWS/LA Gala Benefit at the Pasadena Playhouse; S.T.A.G.E. Benefit at the Luckman Theatre; *The Really Early Dinner Theatre for Kids* at the Hollywood Playhouse; *Boys' Life, Hold Me!, Scruples,* and *Watermelon Boats* at Theatre West; *Mistletoe Mews* at Theatre Geo; and *Is Nudity Required?* at Playhouse of the Foothills.

"I remember performing at family gatherings ever since I was a small child," says Aquino. "I always enjoyed being in the spotlight. To me, acting is like a child's game of pretend, something I always enjoyed. I see it as a career where you can earn a lot of money while having a lot of fun. At the same time you are entertaining people, impacting them, making them think, helping them to feel certain emotions, educating them, and helping them escape from their current lives.

"Most actors who are starting out hold some kind of side job, day job, or part-time job. For me, it was a career in the health care industry working for Kaiser Foundation Health Plan. I then became a health care consultant for one of the Big Six accounting firms, Deloitte & Touche LLP. I was such a good employee that my managers would be flexible and let me go out on auditions.

"After a few years, I realized that I was working too many hours (seventy to eighty per week), and I finally had to make a decision to quit my day job and focus 100 percent of my time toward acting. After booking a few jobs, including a national commercial, I was able to do so. It was a big risk, but one I felt necessary to take. I remember what my acting coach would say: 'Part-time work gets part-time results.' The more I put into acting, the more I got out of it.

"Don't be fooled," stresses Aquino, "acting is a lot of hard work! I am at it seven days a week, mornings, afternoons, evenings, weekends (forty to sixty hours per week). And if I'm not working on the creative side of acting, which is doing my homework for a job that I booked or for an audition, I am working on the business side of acting—talking to my agents and managers, networking, sending my head shots to casting directors, producers, directors, writers, attending seminars, meeting people, etc. I also try to keep my stress level down and take care of myself by getting enough sleep, exercising, eating healthy, and having some relaxation time. And I have been fortunate—the sets I've worked on have all been positive experiences for me.

"What I like most about my work is that I can say that I am making a living doing what I absolutely love to do and that I am pursuing my passion in life. Not too many people in this world can say that. What I like least about my work is that there are a lot of politics in it. It's not always the best actor who gets the job. Some of the time, it's a certain look, what your credits are, who you know, etc., that determines who gets the job. There are a lot of things that are out of your control. That's just part of the business, and you have to accept it.

"I would advise anyone who is considering acting as a career to pursue your dreams and be persistent—but only if it's something you absolutely love to do, and there's nothing else in the world you would rather do. Pursue the creative as well as the business side of acting. Don't let anyone stop you from doing what you want to do. And always keep up your craft, by continuing your training."

Meet Gonzo Schexnayder

Gonzo Schexnayder earned a bachelor's degree in journalism and advertising at Louisiana State University in Baton Rouge. He attended various acting classes at LSU and Monterey Peninsula College in Monterey, California. He attended Chicago's Second City Training Center for more than a year and the Actors Center following that. He is a SAG and AFTRA member.

"I had always wanted to do stand-up comedy but didn't pursue it until graduating from college, when I began working with an improvisational comedy group," explains Schexnayder. "Four months later, the military sent me to Monterey, California, for language training. While there, I did my first staged reading and my first show. I'd never felt such elation as when I performed. Nothing in my life had given me the sheer thrill and rush that I experienced by creating a character and maintaining that throughout a given period of time. Nothing else mattered but that moment on stage, my other actors, and the scene we were performing.

"After completing the language program in November of 1990, I returned to Baton Rouge. There I began the long process of introspection about my career choices and what I wanted to do. I began to audition locally and started reading and studying acting. I still had not made the jump to being an actor; I was merely investigating the possibility.

"One night while watching an interview with John Goodman, I realized how important acting had become to me. I knew that it possibly meant a life of macaroni and cheese, but I knew that up until that moment, nothing had made me as happy or as motivated. While I believe I had the skills and the drive to make it in advertising (or whatever career I chose), I decided that acting was my only logical choice.

"Whether it's rehearsing a show, performing improvisation in front of an audience, or even auditioning for a commercial, it's fun. If you can separate the sense of rejection most actors feel from not getting a part, auditioning for anything becomes your job. Rehearsing becomes your life. Just as a carpenter's job is building a house, as an actor, I look at my job as building my performance. The final product is there for me to look at and admire (if executed well), but the path to that product is the thrill.

"Unfortunately, I'm not at a point in my career where I'm making enough money to quit my day job. I'm close, but not close enough. I still feel the need to have some sense of financial stability, or I lapse into thinking about money. It's all about balance and deciding what's really important. Sure I'd love to have an apartment with central air and a balcony. I'd love to have a car that is still under warranty. But, I know that by putting my efforts and money into my acting career, those other things don't matter. What matters is how it makes me feel. Cars and apartments don't give me the satisfaction that being an actor does.

"How many hours and how busy I am depends on what I'm doing. Over the last year, I've worked with five other actors to open our own theater, Broad Shoulders Theatre, and have found my time constrained. On top of that, I have been pursuing (with some success) a voice-over/on-camera career in addition to working a full-time job. Yesterday I finished six days of shooting on a graduate thesis film, and last weekend we opened our first show (TheatreSports/Chicago, Improvisational Comedy) at our new theater. We have another opening (which I'm not performing in) tonight and expect to open four more shows in the next three months. I've also taken a year of guitar classes and maintained my presence in acting/on-camera classes and workshops. I'm always busy and continually looking for the next chance to market myself and increase my salability as an actor (train, study, perform, work).

"I love the process of acting and sometimes just the fast-paced, eclectic nature of the business. There is always something new to learn and something new to try. The sheer excitement of performing live is amazing, and the personal satisfaction of getting an audience to laugh or cry simply by your words and actions is very gratifying.

"There are many people who take advantage of an actor's desire to perform. As one of the only professions where there is an abundance of people willing to work for nothing—producers, casting directors, agents, and managers who only care about the money will take advantage of and abuse actors for personal gain. Being an astute actor helps prevent much of this, but one must always be on the lookout.

"I would advise others who are interested in this career to work where you are. Perfect your craft. Move when you *have* to—you will know when it's time. And above all, trust your instincts."

Meet Jack Stauffer

Jack Stauffer, a graduate of Northwestern University, has been a working actor since 1968. He created the role of Chuck Tyler in the popular television daytime drama *All My Children* and remained in that role for three and a half years (386 shows). Other regular television appearances include *Battlestar Galactica* and *Young and Restless*. Episodic television appearances include *Lois and Clark, Viper, Designing Women, Quantum Leap, Perfect Strangers, Growing Pains, Knotts Landing,* and *Dynasty*. In all, he has appeared in forty prime-time television shows and numerous movies of the week and miniseries. He was also costar in the movie *Chattanooga Choo Choo*. In theater, he had parts in *My Fair Lady* and *Oliver* at the Grove Theatre in

San Bernadino County. Other play productions include *The Music Man, Annie Get Your Gun, Fiorello, Can Can, Mister Roberts*, and *Guys and Dolls*. His list of achievements also includes parts in more than two hundred commercials.

"I started as a child actor but really didn't become a professional until I graduated from college in 1968," says Stauffer. "I simply sold my car, moved to New York, and hit the pavement!

"I grew up in the industry. My mother worked for Warner Brothers and was W.C. Fields's radio producer. My father produced the *March of Time* for radio during WWII. He then founded his own advertising agency and was responsible for many early television series in the days when the ad agencies had tremendous creative input into a television show. Many notable celebrities used to spend time in our living room. As long as I can remember, I have always wanted to be a performer. It has been my burning desire despite my parents' best efforts to dissuade me from the vagaries of the industry. They would have been happy for me to pursue a more stable and lucrative career.

"Unless you are on a series or are a celebrity, you are constantly battling the belief that you will probably never work again. Thus, your workday consists of looking everywhere and calling anyone who might give you a job. Once you have done all you can do, you inevitably wait for the phone to ring. The vast majority of the time, it doesn't. So, most actors have other jobs—temporary work or selling or, in my case, teaching tennis—anything to make enough money to pay the bills so you can pursue your craft. When you are finally hired for a day or a week or a month or whatever it might be, every moment in your day suddenly has purpose. You get to do what you were meant to do, even if it is only for a short time, or if the part is miniscule. You are on top of the world. Then it is over, and it is back to square one.

"The best thing about your work is the work itself. An actor lives by his or her emotions and the ability to convey them to an audience. A good actor makes it look easy even though it is very hard. That is why so many actors work for free. It is the work that fulfills them. Of course if you get paid, it is much better. The recognition factor is important also. That is why so many actors return to the stage—the gratification is immediate. Any actor who says the applause means nothing is probably lying.

"The worst thing about the industry is that absolute lack of tenure. You are only as good as your next job. Your history, experience, etc., don't mean much. This is because there is no studio system anymore. With no continuity, it is difficult to slowly work your way up the ladder of success. The easiest way to get hired today is to have the executive producer of a hit show as your brother-in-law.

"The question I am asked more than any other is advice on how to get into this industry, and the answer is easy. If you have an absolute, undying, uncontrollable passion to do this—and I mean you will die if you don't—then by all means give it everything you have got. But if you are the slightest bit timid or unsure, choose another career. This is a business based on rejection and it can destroy you. If you sell cars and somebody doesn't buy one, the person simply doesn't want that car. As an actor, when you are turned down, they don't want you. It's difficult not to take it personally. You have to be very strong to keep at it."

Meet Joseph Bowman

Joseph Bowman is an actor in the Los Angeles area. He is a high school graduate who has some college, vocational, and military training. He also participated in the Vanguard Theatre Ensemble Training for four years. He considers himself at the beginning of his acting career.

"I was in the Marine Corps for six years and attained the rank of sergeant via meritorious promotion," says Bowman. "I thoroughly loved the United States Military Corps. It tended to reward a person who acted as if he enjoyed this kind of life, and I was such a person. It seems that I have always been able to act appropriately in any given situation. Older people usually find me charming. Younger people usually find me cool. I love to be the chameleon.

"Five years ago, a friend was attending a model/talent showcase that piqued my interest. I ended up doing it, and he didn't. Even though it was a fiasco, it had revived in me my love of performing.

"At my present level, I do a lot of background work. My military experience gets me a lot of work in productions that have a need for people who have "been there" to add a flavor that normal actors don't always possess. Much of this work involves firing military weapons (blanks) and the knowledge of the safety concerns therein.

"There are not many typical days in acting because every production is very different. It is like working for a different company in a different capacity every day. I may be asked to simply put on a costume and chat (mime) with another actor for eight hours one day. Another day, I might be asked to put on the full battle dress uniform of a branch of the military and fire an M-16 at a monster that isn't there! It varies widely, and that is why I love it.

"The hours and working conditions also vary greatly. Typically, jobs consist of ten-hour days with pleasant working conditions. Sometimes a "shoot" can be as quick as three hours, and sometimes thirteen! It all depends on what the director is looking for and when he or she sees it.

"I enjoy being involved in the artistic side of life. I love the people who populate the arts. They are intelligent, funny, and varied. Nine to five has never been my style. I languish and fade under fluorescent light—ahhh, but shine a spotlight my way and watch me grow ten feet tall and bulletproof.

"I most enjoy the variety and the opportunity to become a character. I have worked my share of day jobs, and I hated the monotony of them. Fame is not my goal. Riches are not my goal. I simply want to do what I love and get paid for it. That is my dream.

"The only thing I don't like about acting is that there is a lot of classism. If you are on a shoot as a background actor, many do not afford you the level of treatment that featured or lead actors enjoy. It is simply a fact of life. Most actors at a high level do not act snobbish to the lowest-rung actors, but many of the production people do.

"I would advise those interested in this field to study the craft and art of acting as if their lives depended upon it. Enjoy life and experience it to the fullest, because good artists bring all their life experiences to their art. Don't let anyone tell you that you are a fool for following your dream. Would you rather be in your rocking chair saying to yourself, 'I wish I had at least tried' or 'I gave it my best shot and had fun along the way'?"

Meet Joe Hansard

Auditioning for a television commercial at the age of five was enough for Joe Hansard to become hooked. He currently works as an actor and a stand-up comedian in New York City. He attended trade school at the Broadcasting Institute of Maryland and has also been an actor-in-residence at the International Film & Television Workshops. Other training includes Stand-Up New York (comedian school) and the Mike Fenton Scene Study Workshop for Film. He has performed his comedy routine at several comedy clubs in New York, and his favorite acting credit is the part of Jimmy Lee Shields in the pilot episode of *Homicide*.

"I've always had a fascination for the motion picture industry," Hansard says. "I enjoy the camaraderie and collaboration that comes with a film or television project, as well as the challenges. I liken it to being in a football game, where you are given the ball, and you run with it. As an actor, I try to expand on the ideas given me by bringing my own uniqueness to a role.

"I like surrounding myself with creative, enthusiastic, and energetic people. There is nothing better than working with folks who truly love their work and get excited about what they do. As a stand-up comedian, nothing is more exhilarating than laughter and applause. It is sweeter than any candy, and it doesn't rot my teeth!

"I owe everything to my mom and dad. I performed at talent showcases in elementary school and was into magic tricks in my preteens. After high school, I didn't know what I wanted to do with my life, and mom came to the rescue again by suggesting a trade school for broadcasting. I was about nineteen or twenty when I landed my first paying gig as a DJ for an A.M. radio station in the college town of Shippensburg, Pennsylvania.

"I got my SAG card when director Christopher Leitch cast me in a principal role in the feature film *The Hitter,* starring Ron O'Neal and Adolph Caesar (who won an Oscar for A *Soldier's Story*).

"I moved to Los Angeles in the early 1980s and had an absolutely horrible experience there. I couldn't get work, had my car repossessed, went bankrupt, and was in poor shape emotionally. It was the darkest time of my life, and there seemed to be no light at the end of the tunnel. But I finally got my act together and moved back east, and that's when Barry Levinson cast me in the pilot episode of *Homicide* on NBC. The "Gone for Goode" episode that I appear in aired after the Superbowl in 1993 and was the highest-rated *Homicide* episode ever.

"I decided to pursue stand-up comedy as a means to network and get myself out there. So far I have performed at Stand-Up New York, the Comedy Store, and the Fun Factory.

"The bulk of my typical day is actually spent looking for work. I track casting leads wherever I can find them, either through personal contacts with the industry professionals I've been associated with over the years, via the Internet, or just the good old grapevine. This is a crazy business. Sometimes it's busy and full beyond belief, and there's barely time to catch my breath. At other times, weeks and even months can go by with nary a job in sight.

"If I'm working on a film or television show, the days are very long—between ten and fourteen hours a day. There is either a real camaraderie that forms on a set or a real paranoia, depending on any number of circumstances and variables in or out of your control that are inherent to the industry. In most cases, it is quite enjoyable, as cast and crew are very professional, and you, more often than not, will get kudos when the director or producer likes the work you are doing. I've found that the entire production and creative team literally evolves into a family.

"I like to work! I love meeting and working with creative, talented actors and directors. I love the business and wouldn't trade it for anything! But the thing I like least is not having any work—having to sit idle. I see an acting coach once a week and take classes to stay tuned up.

"The most important thing is to love your work. Know that there is much competition and some lean times but always remember to enjoy what you do and have fun doing it!"

Music and Dance

"The dance is a poem of which each movement is a word." MATA HARI

Arthur Rubinstein learned the names of the piano keys by the time he was two years old. Ray Charles began to play the piano at age three. Yehudi Menuhin performed solos with the San Francisco Symphony Orchestra at the age of seven. Buddy Holly won $5 singing "Down the River of Memories" at a talent show at five. Gladys Knight won $2,000 singing on the Ted Mack's Amateur Hour at age seven. Marvin Hamlisch was accepted at the Juilliard School of Music at age seven. All of these musical geniuses got their starts very early as those who choose careers in music and dance often do.

Musicians

About 256,000 musicians perform in the United States. Included in this number are those who play in any one of thirty-nine regional, ninety metropolitan, or thirty major symphony orchestras. (Large orchestras employ from 85 to 105 musicians while smaller ones employ 60 to 75 players.) Also counted are members of hundreds of small orchestras, symphony orchestras, pop and jazz groups and those who broadcast or record.

Instrumental musicians may play a variety of musical instruments in an orchestra, popular band, marching band, military band, concert band, symphony, dance band, rock group, or jazz group and may specialize in string, brass, woodwind, or percussion instruments or electronic synthesizers. A large percentage of musicians are proficient in playing several related instruments, such as the flute and clarinet. (This increases employment opportunities.) Those who are very talented have the option to perform as soloists.

Rehearsing and performing take up much of the musicians' time and energy. In addition, musicians, especially those without agents, may need to perform a number of other routine tasks, such as making reservations, keeping track of auditions and/or recordings, arranging for sound effects amplifiers and other equipment to enhance performances, designing lighting, costuming, applying makeup, bookkeeping, and setting up advertising, concerts, tickets, programs, and contracts. Musicians also need to plan the sequence of the numbers to be performed and/or arrange their music according to the conductors' instructions before performances.

Musicians must also keep their instruments clean, polished, tuned, and in proper working order. In addition, they are expected to attend meetings with agents, employers, and conductors or directors to discuss contracts, engagements, and any other business activities.

Performing musicians encompass a wide variety of careers. Here are just a few of the possibilities.

Session Musician

The session musician is the one responsible for playing background music in a studio while a recording artist is singing. The session musician may also be called a freelance musician, backup musician, session player, or studio musician. Session musicians are used for all kinds of recordings, Broadway musicals, operas, rock and folk songs, and pop tunes.

Versatility is the most important ingredient for these professionals—the more instruments the musician has mastered, the greater number of musical styles he or she can offer, the more possibilities for musical assignments. Session musicians often are listed through contractors who call upon them when the need arises. Other possibilities exist through direct requests made by the artists themselves, the group members, or the management team.

The ability to sight-read is important for all musicians, but it is particularly crucial for session musicians. Rehearsal time is usually very limited and costs make it too expensive to have to do retakes.

Section Leader—Section Member

Section members are the individuals who play instruments in an orchestra. They must be talented at playing their instruments of choice and be able to learn the music on their own. Rehearsals are strictly designed for putting all of the instruments and individuals together and for establishing cues such as phrasing and correct breathing. It is expected that all musicians practice sufficiently on their own before rehearsals.

Concertmaster

Those chosen to be concertmasters have the important responsibility of leading the string sections of orchestras during both rehearsals and concerts. In addition, these individuals are responsible for tuning the rest of the orchestra. This is the "music" you hear for about fifteen to twenty seconds before the musicians begin to play the first piece.

Concertmasters must possess leadership abilities and be very knowledgeable of both the music and all the instruments. They answer directly to the conductor.

Floor Show Band Member

Musicians who belong to bands that perform floor shows appear in hotels, nightclubs, cruise ships, bars, concert arenas, and cafes. Usually the bands do two shows per night with a particular number of sets in each show. Additionally, they may be required to play one or two dance sets during the course of the engagement. The audience is seated during the shows and gets up to dance during the dance sets. Shows may include costuming, dialogue, singing, jokes, skits, unusual sound effects, and anything else the band decides to include. Floor show bands may be contracted to appear in one place for one night or several weeks at a time. As expected, a lot of traveling is involved for those who take up this career.

Other Music Professionals

Announcer/Disc Jockey

Announcers play an important role in keeping listeners tuned into a radio or television station. They are the ones who must read messages, commercials, and scripts in entertaining, interesting, and/or enlightening ways. They are also responsible for introducing station breaks, may interview guests, and sell commercial time to advertisers. Sometimes they are called disc jockeys, but actually disc jockeys are the announcers who oversee musical programming at radio stations and during parties, dances, and other special occasions.

Disc jockeys may also interview guests and make public service announcements, announce the time, do the weather forecast, or even report the news. They must be very knowledgeable about music in general and all aspects of their specialties, specifically the music and the groups who play and/or sing that kind of music. Their programs may feature general music, rock, pop, country and western, or any specific musical period or style, such as tunes from the 1950s or 1960s.

Since radio programs are usually performed live, disc jockeys must be quick thinking and personable. Most often they do not have a written script to simply read. They also must be able to perform well under stress and in situations where things do not go as planned. Thus, the best disc jockeys possess pleasant, soothing voices and good wit and are able to keep listeners fully entertained.

It takes considerable skills to work the radio controls, watch the clock, select music, talk with someone, and be entertaining to the audience, all at the same time.

Conductor and Choral Director

The music conductor is the director for all of the performers in a musical presentation, whether it be singing or instrumental. Though there are many types of conductors—symphony, choral groups, dance bands, opera, matching bands, and ballet—in all cases, the music conductor is in charge of interpreting the music.

Conductors audition and select musicians, choose the music to accommodate the talents and abilities of the musicians, and direct rehearsals and performances, applying conducting techniques to achieve desired musical effects like harmony, rhythm, tempo, and shading.

Orchestral conductors lead instrumental music groups, such as orchestras, dance bands, and various popular ensembles. Choral directors lead choirs and glee clubs, sometimes working with a band or orchestra conductor.

Training for Musicians

Many people who become professional musicians begin studying an instrument at an early age. They may gain valuable experience playing in school or community bands or orchestras or with friends. Singers usually start training when their voices mature. Participation in school musicals or in a choir often provides good early training and experience.

Musicians need extensive and prolonged training to acquire the necessary skills, knowledge, and ability to interpret music. This training may be obtained through private study with an accomplished musician, in a college or university music program, in a music conservatory, or through practice with a group. For study in an institution, an audition frequently is necessary. Formal courses include musical theory, music interpretation, composition, conducting, and instrumental and voice instruction. Composers, conductors, and arrangers need advanced training in these subjects as well.

Many colleges, universities, and music conservatories grant bachelor's or graduate degrees in music. Many also grant degrees in music education to qualify graduates for a state certificate to teach music in an elementary or secondary school.

Those who perform popular music must have an understanding of and feeling for the styles of music that interest them, but classical training can expand their employment opportunities, as well as their musical abilities.

Although voice training is an asset for singers of popular music, many with untrained voices have successful careers. As a rule, musicians take lessons with private teachers when young and seize every opportunity to make amateur or professional appearances.

Desirable Personal Qualities

Young people who are considering careers in music should have musical talent, versatility, creative ability, poise, and the stage presence to face large audiences. Since quality performance requires constant study and practice, self-discipline is vital. Moreover, musicians who play concert and nightclub engagements must have physical stamina because frequent travel and night performances are required. They must also be prepared to face the anxiety of intermittent employment and rejections when auditioning for work.

Earnings for Musicians

Earnings for musicians often depend on a performer's professional reputation and place of employment and on the number of hours worked. The most successful musicians can earn far more than the minimum salaries indicated below.

According to the American Federation of Musicians, minimum salaries in major orchestras range from about $1,000 to $1,200 per week during the performing season. Each orchestra works out a separate contract with its members. The season of these top orchestras range from forty-eight to fifty-two weeks, with most being fifty-two weeks. In regional orchestras, the minimum salaries are between $400 and $700 per week, and the seasons last twenty-five to thirty-eight weeks, with an average of thirty weeks. Some now work a fifty-two-week season. Community orchestras, however, have more limited levels of funding and offer salaries that are much lower for seasons of shorter duration.

Musicians employed in motion picture or television recording and those employed by recording companies are paid a minimum ranging from about $200 to $260 a week, depending on the size of the ensemble.

Musicians employed by some symphony orchestras work under master wage agreements, which guarantee a season's work up to fifty-two weeks. Many other musicians may face relatively long periods of unemployment between jobs. Even when employed, however, many work part-time. Thus, their earnings generally are lower than those in many other occupations. Moreover, since they may not work steadily for one employer, some performers cannot qualify for unemployment compensation, and few have either sick leave or vacations with pay. For these reasons, many musicians give private lessons or take jobs unrelated to music to supplement their earnings as performers.

Many musicians belong to a local of the American Federation of Musicians. Professional singers usually belong to a branch of the Associated Actors and Artists of America.

Dancers

Ever since ancient times, dancers have expressed ideas, stories, rhythm, and sound with their bodies. In addition to being an art form for its own sake, dance also complements opera, musical comedy, television, movies, music videos, and commercials. Therefore, many dancers sing and act, as well as dance.

Dancers most often perform as a group, although a few top artists dance solo. Many dancers combine stage work with teaching or choreographing.

Choreographers

Choreographers create original dances. They may also create new interpretations to traditional dances, like the ballet *Nutcracker*, since few dances are written down. Choreographers instruct performers at rehearsals to achieve the desired effect. They also audition performers.

Ballet Dancers

Ballet dancing requires a lot of training—in fact, more than any other kind of dancing. Ballet dancers are performers who express a theme or story.

Modern Dancers

Modern dancers use bodily movements and facial expressions to express ideas and moods. Jazz is an example of a modern dance.

Tap Dancers

Tap dancers use tap shoes to keep in time with all kinds of music. The shoes allow them to tap out various dance rhythms.

The Life of a Dancer

Dancing is strenuous. Rehearsals require very long hours and usually take place daily, including weekends and holidays. For shows on the road, weekend travel is often necessary. Rehearsals and practice are generally scheduled during the day. Since most performances take place in the evening, dancers must usually work late hours.

Due to the physical demands, most dancers stop performing by their late thirties, but they sometimes continue to work in the dance field as choreographers, dance teachers and coaches, or as artistic directors. Some celebrated dancers, however, continue performing beyond the age of fifty.

Dancers work in a variety of settings, including eating and drinking establishments, theatrical and television productions, dance studios and schools, dance companies and bands, and amusement parks. In addition, there are many dance instructors in secondary schools, colleges and universities, and private studios. Many teachers also perform from time to time.

New York City is the home of many of the major dance companies. Other cities with full-time professional dance companies include Atlanta, Boston, Chicago, Cincinnati, Cleveland, Columbus, Dallas, Houston, Miami, Milwaukee, Philadelphia, Pittsburgh, Salt Lake City, San Francisco, Seattle, and Washington, D.C.

Training for Dancers

Training for dancers varies according to the type of dance. Early ballet training for women usually begins at five to eight years of age and is often given by private teachers and independent ballet schools. Serious training traditionally begins between the ages of ten and twelve. Men often begin their training between the ages of ten and fifteen.

Students who demonstrate potential in the early teens receive more intensive and advanced professional training at regional ballet schools or schools conducted under the auspices of the major ballet companies.

Leading dance school companies often have summer training programs from which they select candidates for admission to their regular full-time training programs. Most dancers have their professional auditions by age seventeen or eighteen; however, training and practice never end. Professional ballet dancers have one to one and one-half hours of lessons every day and spend many additional hours practicing and rehearsing.

Early and intensive training also is important for the modern dancer, but modern dance generally does not require as many years of training as ballet.

Because of the strenuous and time-consuming training required, a dancer's formal academic instruction may be minimal. However, a broad, general education including music, literature, history, and the visual arts is helpful in the interpretation of dramatic episodes, ideas, and feelings.

Many colleges and universities offer bachelor's or graduate degrees in dance. This might be through the departments of music, physical education, fine arts, or theater. Most programs concentrate on modern dance but also offer courses in ballet/classical techniques, dance composition, dance history, dance criticism, and movement analysis.

A college education is not essential to obtaining employment as a professional dancer. In fact, ballet dancers who postpone their first auditions until graduation may compete at a disadvantage with younger dancers. On the other hand, a college degree can help the dancer who retires at an early age, as often happens, and wishes to enter another field of work.

Completion of a college program in dance and education is essential to qualify for employment as a college, high school, or elementary dance teacher. Colleges, as well as conservatories, generally require graduate degrees, but performance experience often may be substituted. However, a college background is not necessary for teaching dance or choreographing professionally. Studio schools usually require teachers to have experience as performers.

Earnings for Dancers

The earnings for many professional dancers is governed by union contracts. Dancers in major opera ballets, classical ballets, and modern dance corps belong to the American Guild of Musical Artists, Inc., AFL-CIO. Those on live or videotaped television belong to the American Federation of Television and Radio Artists. Those who perform in films and on television belong to the Screen Actors Guild or the Screen Extras Guild. Those in musical comedies are members of the Actors Equity Association. The unions and producers sign basic agreements specifying minimum salary rates, hours of work, benefits, and other conditions of employment. However, the contract each dancer signs with the producer of the show may be more favorable than the basic agreement.

The minimum weekly salary for dancers in ballet and modern productions is about $610. According to the American Guild of Musical Artists, new first-year dancers being paid for single performances under a union agreement earn about $475 per week and $70 per rehearsal hour. Dancers on tour receive an

additional allowance for room and board. The minimum performance rate for dancers in theatrical motion pictures is about
$100 per day of filming. The normal workweek is thirty hours,
including rehearsals and matinee and evening performances, but
may be longer. Extra compensation is paid for additional hours
worked.

Earnings from dancing are generally low because dancers'
employment is irregular. They often must supplement their
income by taking temporary jobs unrelated to dancing.

Dancers covered by union contracts are entitled to some paid
sick leave, paid vacations, and various health and pension benefits, including extended sick pay and childbirth provisions, provided by their unions. Employers contribute toward these
benefits. Most other dancers do not receive any benefits.

Earnings of choreographers vary greatly. Earnings from fees
and performance royalties range from about $970 a week in small
professional theaters to more than $30,000 for an eight- to ten-
week rehearsal period for a Broadway production. In high-bud-
get films, choreographers make $3,000 for a five-day week; in
television, $7,500 to $10,000 for up to fourteen workdays.

Meet Some Music Professionals

Meet Mark Marek

Mark Marek is a singer and the owner of Private Stock Variety
Dance Band of Lenexa, Kansas. His background includes two
years of college with course work focusing on music theory, audio
and engineering, and the fundamentals of music and business.

"I started playing the drums in junior high school and then
learned how to play the six-string guitar," says Marek. "By the
time I was sixteen, my brother had his own band, so I started

playing and learning about bands from him. Fourteen years ago, I started my own band.

"My band is primarily a country club/high-dollar type band. We play mostly at weddings, country clubs, and other formal occasions. The band's working hours are usually 6:30 P.M. until 1:00 A.M., mostly on Friday and Saturday. Most gigs usually last three to four hours, and we have to arrive there at least an hour and a half before the start time. We generally do one-hour sets, with a twenty-minute break every hour or so. In addition to setting up, we also have to break down the equipment. Because we've been together for so long, we don't need to rehearse much, perhaps every three to four months.

"I love seeing the reaction of the audience. It's fun to know and see that they are having a good time. That's the thrill I get out of it.

"What I least like is the inconsistency in bookings. Each month, the number of gigs changes, which affects the cash flow. The peak periods for the band are December and May/June.

"During the week, I mostly take bookings, spend time on the phone getting the specifics for each one, and contact the five band members about our schedule. I also handle all of the contracts for each performance. Aside from the band, I also give private guitar lessons and book gigs for other bands.

"To approach success in the music industry, you need to have good people skills, a general sense of business, a real enjoyment for what you do, a recognition of what your niche is in the music world, patience, good customer relations skills, expert technical skills, and a knowledge of audio and video.

"Having a band is a business, not an ego trip. You really need to have a basic knowledge of business and marketing. You can be the best musician, but you have to know how to sell yourself in order to be successful. It's a tough way to make a living. That's why you have to really have a passion for the business."

Meet Priscilla Gale

Soprano Priscilla Gale attended both the Juilliard School of Music and the Cleveland Institute of Music. She has also studied in Austria and with private teachers Luigi Ricci (in Rome) and Michael Trimble. Currently, when she's not performing with an opera company or symphony orchestra, she is a faculty member at Wesleyan University in Middletown, Connecticut, where she teaches voice.

"Having come from a very musical family of pianists, singers, and violinists, I was at the piano at the age of five," says Gale. "My family always assumed that I would pursue a career as a pianist, but I realized my real joy and fulfillment was in singing, not the piano. As I began to explore that world more thoroughly, I discovered opera, and I found my home. The rest is history. I received my first professional contract with the Ft. Wayne (Indiana) Symphony Orchestra during my senior year at Cleveland Institute of Music.

"Every engagement a singer/performer experiences changes you in the most wonderful way. You, as an artist, grow on multiple levels—personally, artistically—and one thing leads to another. Each time, your life as an artist is changed; you grow in some immeasurable, wonderful way, and the possibilities are limitless.

"No one job site is like another. In opera, the rehearsals are intense, with the appropriate union breaks but with long, long days, usually over a ten- to twelve-hour period daily, and over two weeks or perhaps three. It really depends on how a company works, and they all work differently.

"Orchestra jobs tend to be over a three- or four-day period. Usually you have a piano rehearsal with the conductor. Then there are one or two orchestra rehearsals, followed by the performances. It is always busy and intense, but exciting. It is fast paced, and one must know one's craft. There is little room for poor preparation. And, you must always have the ability to adjust to every circumstance and environment, for no two are ever the same. Every conductor is different, every director, etc. You must be very adaptable and professional.

"What I love most about my work is the ability to touch an audience—people I never meet individually but collectively. My heart and soul meets theirs. But there are just not enough performance opportunities for everyone, and it is no longer possible to make a full-time living at this career, unless you are one of the lucky top 20 percent.

"I always tell people who want to do this kind of work to look inward and ask if there is anything else in life that will bring them happiness and fulfillment. If so, then I suggest that they do that instead. If not, then they should by all means pursue this career. But know that it is—especially in the beginning—a very complicated business that represents a difficult life.

"Talent is but a small piece of it. Most people cannot comprehend the level of sacrifice that this career requires. There is that wonderful, romantic notion of being the starving artist, but there's nothing romantic about it when you're living it.

"However, with hard work, determination, perseverance, and an unwavering faith in yourself, anything can happen. The journey is an incredible ride, and one I would not have missed. And as I look back at my past, at my present, and toward my future, I can honestly say that I am one of the lucky ones."

Meet Karen Tyler

Karen Tyler of Austin, Texas, earned an associate of arts degree from Pepperdine University. She has been working as a blues singer/songwriter/guitarist since 1979.

"I had a natural talent for singing and found songwriting to be an incredible emotional outlet," says Tyler. "And I have developed some pretty good business skills in order to stay in the music business. From the beginning, being front and center stage and being appreciated for my feelings was important to me.

"Many artists have to have day jobs to support their music, making it very difficult to actually have the time to write, record, and do live performances. My husband and I moved to Texas so that we could afford to live on one salary while I pursued my music. Since he is also my bass player, my studio engineer/producer, and maker and repairer of guitars, he, of course, benefits from any of my successes.

"I get up fairly early each day and start to work by 9 or 10 A.M.," she says. "I have so many tasks to accomplish! I keep a mailing list and create all of my own promotional materials via the computer and a couple of printers. I am responsible for all of the bookkeeping and accounting of band income and CD and tape sales. I write a quarterly newsletter. I also make demo tapes and mail out promotional packages almost constantly. I do tons of research on radio stations, booking agents, clubs, festivals, record companies, and the like. I read everything I can get my hands on about the music business and the blues. I spend anywhere from one to four hours a day doing just the business of music. In addition, I play several nights a week from two to four hours, sometimes traveling three and four hours to play. Nothing at all may happen for a period of time, and, just when I get into a routine I really like, someone will call or an opportunity will arise that will take all of my attention.

"There is never a time when something like songwriting or practicing guitar doesn't take a back seat to some kind of business duty. I have tried to get a manager but have had some really bad experiences and at this point in my career feel that it is better if I retain the control of my career even if the responsibilities are a bit overwhelming. Everyone always has a suggestion about what you should be doing to help your career. And you can't possibly do everything people suggest, so making an action plan and sticking to it is the best thing. Trying to be organized is my biggest challenge and getting things down on paper helps.

"I spend anywhere from twenty-five to thirty hours a week doing music business and play anywhere from four to twelve hours a week. I work from a home office, and so it gets a little lonely. My husband is moving his office into the home, which I

assume will make it a bit better for me. At least I will have someone to bounce some ideas off. Sometimes I really feel like I'm out
there all alone.

"I enjoy a good crowd response to my music. It makes it all
worthwhile when someone comes up and tells me I have an
amazing voice or that I play the guitar well or that a certain song
really touched them. The worst part is probably that people don't
go out as much as they used to. They are programmed by television, radio, and print media as to what to buy and what to listen
to or go to see. They get comfortable going to hear certain acts,
and, until they have heard rave reviews about some artists forty
or fifty times, they don't make the effort to go and see them.
Even when they do, they are liable to slip back into the habit of
going where they always go. A side effect is that talent doesn't
count as much as who you know and how much fun you are to
hang out with.

"On top of that, bands who want to make it are expected to
finance their own recordings, put out expensive CDs, and sell literally thousands of them before a record company will consider
signing them. This is kind of hard when you are playing for fewer
and fewer people every day.

"I would advise those interested in this career to go to college
and develop a talent (preferably nonmusical) so you can create
your own business—computers, catering, consulting (it really
doesn't have to start with a "C" though). You have to have some
way of supporting yourself and coming up with $5,000 to
$10,000 every year or two for a CD, and you have to have a flex-
ible schedule so that you can tour and support the CD and work
whenever you can."

Meet Kathryn Maffei

Kathryn Maffei has been playing the piano for more than forty
years. She has ten years of classical training through a concert
pianist. "When I started taking piano lessons at eight years old,"

says Maffei, "I began to entertain my family. Then I performed for family and friends' parties, as well as local club and organization events. Quickly it spread to playing the piano for chorus classes in grammar school, high school, and bands and entertaining for many different kinds of local events, such as proms, fashion shows, variety shows, plays, and other social functions.

"I got married and took a few years off to raise my family. When my children were of preschool and kindergarten age, I went to school with them and did music classes for their teachers because they did not play the piano or have live music for their classes. I became the church organist in communities in which we lived and played for weddings, funerals, and masses.

"Once I was heard by others, it quickly spread to doing parties at hotels, country clubs, Christmas parties, birthday parties, anniversaries, class reunions, etc. I became music director for a performing arts company in my area, and I have been piano conductor for more than a dozen musical plays, including *Oliver, Annie, Big River, Hello Dolly, Bye Bye Birdie, Peter Pan, You're a Good Man, Charlie Brown,* and *Beauty and the Beast.*

"I have provided the music for local beauty pageants, concerts in the park, and Fourth of July pageants. I have performed for many benefits to raise money for projects in our community and, most recently, played for a religious concert. I have also served as a judge for music talent in our area. Currently, I teach thirty-two private piano students, and I am the church pianist/organist as well.

"I began working at Our Lady of Miracles Catholic School in Gustine, California, a private Catholic school, eight years ago, and I now work three days a week teaching music classes from kindergarten through eighth grade. This came about after the assistant superintendent of schools saw me at work and hired me immediately to do music at her school. Most recently, I was appointed to a visual and performing arts committee to integrate performing arts in the schools in our diocese.

"When designing music programs for children, my main concern is to teach a love for the art of music. I believe it is best done at the earliest age possible, for a love for music and performing arts will stay with children all their lives, as it did in mine. It is well known that bringing music and liberal arts to students is important on so many levels and ensures a broad and rich education. It reinforces social skills, positive attitudes, and values and supports growth and intellectual enrichment. The value of the arts serves not only to develop personal intellectual growth, but also sharpens judgment and interpersonal decision making. The key is to start with young children, and I know almost no other way to get and keep a small child's attention than with music.

"I truly love children and music. I have never been sorry I perform in public. I get so much enjoyment out of it. It is my life's work as much as an accountant who works with numbers and lawyers who work with laws! To others I say: Go for it if you feel it is in your heart!"

Meet Mike Watson

Mike Watson, head of Watson Entertainment, Inc., is a recording artist at Uniworld Records in Atlanta, Georgia. He attended West Georgia College and majored in music.

"I started playing professionally in 1980 as lead guitarist and harmony singer for a band on the circuit," explains Watson. "I have been fascinated with music as long as I can remember, and I turned that dream into reality with a lot of hard work and perseverance and never settling for second best or taking no for an answer.

"When I'm playing in town, a typical day is the following—I rise about noon and do everyday things like cutting grass, etc. Then, I work at the club from 9 P.M. until 1 or 2 A.M. Entertaining is what I do. Naturally, it is always a party atmosphere. When I go to different states doing shows, it's somewhat similar, except

I get to see places and people in one day I probably will never meet and maybe not see again.

"I love almost every part of my job. I consider myself to be so fortunate because I am able to do the one thing I love doing most—making a living at making music. My least favorite part is dealing with people who had a little too much to drink and every now and then having to deal with less than desirable booking agents who send you to a job that isn't quite what they paint it to be.

"My advice to others is, if you have a genuine dream, never give up! If you know in your heart you have what it takes to succeed in your chosen profession, go for it!"

Meet Rudy Gonzales

Rudy Gonzales is a "Cowboy Poet and Western Humorist" who travels all over the United States and Canada, performing his original and traditional cowboy poetry and songs at conventions, rodeos, fairs, banquets, and other gatherings. He is the founder and director of the Idaho State Cowboy Poetry Gathering, now in its eleventh year, and also publishes the *American Cowboy Poet Magazine*. Additionally, he has written and produced two videos of his performances, "The Liar's Hour" and "Cowboy Poetry Live." Though he has shared his poetry and music with literally thousands of people, Rudy says that two of his most famous audience members were former President Gerald Ford and former Vice President Dan Quayle.

When he's not busy traveling and performing, Rudy lives the cowboy life with his wife, Rose, on their small ranch in Idaho. He grew up on a ranch in Colorado and now uses that lifelong experience to be a rancher, horse trainer instructor, and instructor of farrier science (horseshoeing). "In one form or another, I have been doing what I do ever since I can remember," says Gonzales. "And it's what I want to do.

"I grew up in the cattle business. My father was a sought-after horse trainer and farrier. I spent more than thirty years in the marketing field as the national sales manager for a Texas meat company. But none of the values of today's society appeal to me. I threw it all away to go back to a cowboy life. Then, the entertainment business came calling on me. I have always enjoyed entertaining people and making them laugh.

"I have a home office at my ranch in Idaho. The atmosphere is warm, but busy. Feeding livestock is the first order of my day, but then I turn my attention to the phone. Calls usually start very early. Negotiations for shows seem to occupy most of the day between calls and faxed agreements. Many performances come mid-week, and weekends generally find me out of town performing."

Meet Chris Murphy

Chris Murphy is a professional musician, entertainer, record producer, and entertainment buyer, as well as a part-time disc jockey at a college radio station. He began music lessons as a teenager and later attended Berklee College of Music in Boston. His father was also a musician, and Chris often played in bands with him before going on the road with his own band in 1978.

"I don't know how to do anything else," says Murphy. "Music is one of the few things I was good at and could take pride in. As a teenager, I felt that music stood out as something that was fun and that I excelled at. I started playing the saxophone at age seventeen and started playing in bands about the same time. I was in love with the blues long before I became a blues musician."

"My work atmosphere is great. I play in blues clubs four to six nights a week. I also spend at least an hour a day on the phone, organizing gigs and musicians. I meet a lot of interesting, talented, and funny people. I receive a lot of respect and love from the audiences I perform for. There is nothing that can replace the feeling of being onstage with a great band on a good night! I also have time to spend with my daughter in the daytime during the week, though occasionally I am away for the weekend. I enjoy the fact that when I go out to earn money, I am going out to play. How many people can say that?

"My advice is to never ever quit. The people who hang in there are the ones who inherit the entertainment business!"

Meet Lionel Ward

Lionel Ward first became interested in being a musician when he was only nine years old and his mother bought him an Airline guitar for Christmas. Now he tours North America and Europe as the lead singer for the New World Band, a music group that entertains audiences with classic and contemporary rock and country songs.

Lionel was discovered by the late Wolfman Jack, who noticed Lionel's resemblance to Elvis Presley and invited him to a meeting. (Even now, the band ends each performance with a tribute to Elvis.) Lionel's manager then sent a demo tape to Wolfman Jack's record label, Sonic Records, Inc., and the New World Band began recording under the Sonic label.

"I came from a musical family, so there was always music in the house," Ward says. "Music is therapy for the soul. It is the greatest feeling in the world to be able to play in front of an audience and see the enjoyment you give them. If you can relieve them of the everyday burdens of life for just a few minutes, you've done something important. The natural high you get from doing a live show cannot be compared to anything else. The only way you can achieve this feeling is through the music. And the beautiful thing is that it is all natural. Being able to sing and play an instrument is a God-given talent; you cannot buy this anywhere. You have to be born with it. It is a blessing to be able to share it with your audience.

"One thing I learned very early in the entertainment business is that every performance has to be the best you can possibly do. The key is to be able to sing your songs like they are being performed for the very first time. It may actually be the thousandth time you have sung that song, but, in my opinion, it should be a thousand times better than the first. The people in the audience have chosen to take the time out of their evening to come and hear you play. You do not want to disappoint them, and I always make sure I do my very best whether there are five people in the audience or five thousand.

"My job as lead singer is to ensure that all arrangements have been made for the band. How big is the stage? How much room do I have to move around? The size of the show will tell us which public address system we are going to use for the evening. What lighting system is going to be used? How many people are we going to need for the road crew? I must ensure that all of this is taken care of, because it affects my show tremendously if I cannot hear the band or we can't see because someone forgot to put up a spotlight.

"As far as what work I actually do, I am involved with every aspect, right down to the last microphone sound check. You cannot measure how many hours are involved because some shows take days. If you count the actual rehearsal time, driving to the gigs, setup and teardown times, and sound checks, you would think we were insane. Our lives are devoted to music, but it is a labor of love. Sometimes we are gone from our homes for weeks. Living in hotels, doing radio and television interviews, is not one big party. I am very fortunate because for as long as I have been doing this, I have never considered it work. I truly love what I am doing.

"I love recording in the studio. It is like taking a piece of your life and freezing it in time. But I also love performing live. Again, there is no better feeling in the world than when the audience is wrapped up in your song, and you are taking them on a journey.

Sometimes I get so involved in the show that when I open my eyes, everyone is standing and cheering with tears in their eyes. It is then that I know they have felt the same things I have in the song.

"There is no downside in this business as far as I'm concerned. I am very fortunate that my wife travels with me and shares my dreams. For some people, I think a downside would be having to leave their family.

"My advice to others is to follow your dreams and what you feel in your heart. This business is very rough and unforgiving at times. But if you believe in yourself, and you have the burning desire to make it, then you will. This business cannot be measured by hours or even days. It cannot be measured by money, either, though we need money to survive. If you truly believe in yourself and your music, everything else will fall into place.

"Many times you will hear me thank the audience for their support through the years. I was born a poor boy—rich with love and dreams, though—and I am definitely living my dreams!"

Meet John A. Roberts

John A. Roberts attended Montgomery College, Rockville campus, majoring in speech and drama. He then attended the University of Maryland at College Park, majoring in radio and television.

In August of 1996, he competed in the National DJ of the Year competition in Atlantic City and was ranked among the top ten DJs nationally. In January of 1997, he was awarded the Best Club DJ of 1996 in Las Vegas by the American DJ awards. He has spoken at numerous DJ conventions and expos nationally and in Canada and has written articles for magazines like *Mobile Beat*, *DJ Times*, and the *ADJA News*."

"I started as a stand-up comic in the late sixties to mid-seventies," says Roberts. "I learned from the school of hard knocks, as I was one of the first in this profession. While in the U.S. Air Force I competed in the talent show, Tops in Blue. I won first place in comedy and went on to worldwide competition.

"Currently I am owner of John Roberts' Roving Records—my personal DJ and karaoke service. I am also founder and national operations manager of the American Disc Jockey Association and owner of The DJ Training Center, the nation's first full-service independent training facility.

"I started working as a DJ while still in the air force, at the USO club in Washington, D.C., in 1973. In 1975, when I was about to get out of the service, I had this totally unique idea. I would be like a band and play music at clubs, weddings, and parties, yet I would be a DJ and play records. I could go anywhere, be mobile! I had absolutely no idea that someone else might have this idea, too. I certainly had never heard of it and knew of no one who did it. Many people close to me thought I was crazy and should pursue a real job. No one knew disco was brewing right around the corner! That's when DJs truly became accepted as a form of entertainment.

"I always wanted to get into broadcasting and wanted to keep up with my comedy. I figured this could be a stepping-stone in both directions. But after doing stand-up comedy and doing stage shows in high school and college, I loved the live audience.

"In radio you played to a wall. In a club or party, I was playing to live people and could feel the people and see their instant reaction to things I did. It was totally spontaneous. This is what attracted me to this particular format of entertainment. I could be self-employed and fulfill the American dream doing something I really loved. How many people can say that every time they work it's a party!

"But it's also a business and must be treated as such. There are legal ramifications inasmuch as we deal with contracts. There is a responsibility there. Music and supplies must be ordered and maintained. Keeping up with music is a major expense. These are the tools of the trade. Equipment must be purchased and maintained. There are promotions, marketing, advertising, hiring, firing, bookkeeping, and all the other normal procedures that any office or business encompasses.

"My days are busy. I am responsible for answering phones and handling customer inquiries, performing the negotiations and attending to contracts, training and scheduling DJs, ordering supplies and music, promoting the business, making advertising decisions, cataloging music, and creating and printing our karaoke catalogues.

"Then at night I will perform at a party. This requires more than just playing music. DJs work as coordinators between the host and guests. We take requests from partygoers and, in general, try to keep everyone involved and happy.

"What I like most of this career is that I am my own boss. I can pick and choose the shows I do. I get to work in exciting places and meet exciting, sometimes famous people. Being a mobile DJ has lead to some interesting job opportunities for me. I did a television show like American Bandstand for more than three years. I was a part of more than thirty to forty radio and television commercials, performed on radio, was one of the original hosts of the Home Shopper's Club of Virginia, auditioned for a movie, and have been able to travel all over the United States.

"On the downside, there are no benefits that you ordinarily receive from an employer (unless you are willing to pay for them). It's very hard on my personal social life. My average time to get to sleep is three to four in the morning.

"My advice is that people should realize that this is a business and that it must be treated as such. I'd advise others to never burn bridges. Create friendly competitors and network, network, network. Learn to entertain, think on your feet. Even though we play records (CDs) and other people's music, we still are entertainers. Always be willing to learn new tricks and techniques to stay on top. The minute you think you know it all is the minute your competition starts getting ahead of you."

Meet Sean M. Meaney

Sean M. Meaney is owner of Sterling Entertainment of Tempe, Arizona. "I started in the music business in 1984," says Meaney. "When I first started doing this," Meaney says, "I couldn't believe that people would pay me to perform at parties. (Of course, I was only fifteen at the time.) A few years later, I got my first chance to work in a nightclub. With people asking me to do private parties, it just took off. The hardest part was learning about equipment. I did not go to school for any technical training, so it was all done by trial and error.

"After fourteen years, my love for performing has evolved into a company that performs at weddings, Bar/Bat Mitzvahs, and corporate events. And I still learn new things every day.

"We are one of the few DJ entertainment companies that do this full-time. During the week, there is a lot of office work. That involves booking jobs, going to meet clients, and finding new ways to entertain people. A day starts off in the office, working on different marketing ideas. If there are no clients to see, I continue to pursue these efforts all day. On Friday, we get ready for the weekend. That includes getting all of the equipment ready for the DJs. We want to make sure that everything is all set.

"Some seasons are busier than others. The wedding season is always a hectic one. Besides running the office, I still go out to do shows. All together, I put in about sixty-plus hours per week.

"My favorite part of this job remains my love for entertaining. And I enjoy working for myself. On the downside, it is very difficult to find reliable people to hire to do shows. Also, running your own company is not easy.

"My advice to others is to set your goals and stick to that path. There are many areas in this business to go into—just pick one and proceed!"

For More Information

Acting

Information about opportunities in regional theaters may be obtained from:

Theatre Communications Group, Inc.
355 Lexington Avenue
New York, NY 10017

A directory of theatrical programs may be purchased from:

National Association of Schools of Theatre
11250 Roger Bacon Drive, Suite 21,
Reston, VA 22090

Additional information may be secured from the following associations:

Actors Equity Association
165 West Forty-sixth Street
New York, NY 10036

Alliance of Canadian Cinema
Television and Radio Artists
2239 Yonge Street
Toronto, Ontario M5S 2B5
Canada

Alliance of Resident Theaters/New York
325 Spring Street
New York, NY 10013

American Federation of Television and Radio Artists (AFTRA)
260 Madison Avenue
New York, NY 10016

American Film Institute
P.O. Box 27999
2021 North Western Avenue
Los Angeles, CA 90027

American Guild of Variety Artists (AVA)
184 Fifth Avenue
New York, NY 10019

American Theater Association (ATA)
1010 Wisconsin Avenue NW
Washington, DC 20007

American Theatre Works, Inc.
Theatre Directories
P.O. Box 519
Dorset, VT 05251

Canadian Actors Equity Association
260 Richmond Street East
Toronto, Ontario M5A 1P4
Canada

National Arts Jobbank
141 East Palace Avenue
Santa Fe, NM 87501

National Association of Schools of Theatre
11250 Roger Bacon Drive, Suite 21
Reston, VA 22090

Screen Actors Guild (SAG)
5757 Wilshire Boulevard
Los Angeles, CA 90036

Music and Dance

There are literally hundreds of professional associations for musicians and dancers. Contact any of the following organizations for more information about employment in this field.

American Choral Directors Association (ACDA)
P.O. Box 6310
Lawton, OK 73506

American Federation of Musicians (AFM)
1501 Broadway, Suite 600
New York, NY 10036

American Federation of Television and Radio Artists (AFTRA)
260 Madison Avenue
New York, NY 10016

American Guild of Musical Artists (AGMA)
1727 Broadway
New York, NY 10019

American Guild of Organists (AGO)
475 Riverside Drive, Suite 1260
New York, NY 10115

American Guild of Music (AGM)
5354 Washington Street
Box 3
Downers Grove, IL 60515

American Federation of Musicians
1501 Broadway, Suite 600
New York, NY 10036

American Music Conference (AMC)
5140 Avenida Encinas
Carlsbad, CA 92008

American Musicological Society
201 South Thirty-fourth Street
University of Pennsylvania
Philadelphia, PA 19104

American Symphony Orchestra League (ASOL)
777 Fourteenth Street NW, Suite 500
Washington, DC 20005

Academy of Country Music (ACM)
500 Sunnyside Boulevard
Woodbury, NY 11797

Association of Canadian Orchestras
56 The Esplanade, Suite 311
Toronto, Ontario M5E IA7
Canada

Black Music Association (BMA)
1775 Broadway
New York, NY 10019

Broadcast Education Association
National Association of Broadcasters
1771 N Street NW
Washington, DC 20036

Broadcast Music, Inc. (BMI)
320 West Fifty-seventh Street
New York, NY 10019

Chamber Music America
545 Eighth Avenue
New York, NY 10018

Chorus America
Association of Professional Vocal Ensembles
2111 Sansom Street
Philadelphia, PA 19103

College Music Society
202 West Spruce
Missoula, MT 59802

Concert Artists Guild (CAG)
850 Seventh Avenue
Room 1003
New York, NY 10019

Country Music Association (CMA)
P.O. Box 22299
One Music Circle South
Nashville, TN 37203

Gospel Music Association (GMA)
P.O. Box 23201
Nashville, TN 37202

International Conference of Symphony and Opera Musicians
    (ICSOM)
6607 Waterman
St. Louis, MO 63130

Metropolitan Opera Association (MOA)
Lincoln Center
New York NY 10023

National Academy of Popular Music (NAPM)
885 Second Avenue
New York, NY 10017

National Academy of Recording Arts and Sciences (NARAS)
303 North Glen Oaks Boulevard, Suite 140
Burbank, CA 91502

National Association of Music Theaters
John F. Kennedy Center
Washington, DC 20566

National Association of Schools of Music
11250 Roger Bacon Drive, Suite 21
Reston, VA 22091

National Orchestral Association (NOA)
474 Riverside Drive, Room 455
New York, NY 10115

National Symphony Orchestra Association (NSOA)
JFK Center for the Performing Arts
Washington, DC 20566

Opera America
777 Fourteenth Street NW, Suite 520
Washington, DC 20005

Radio-Television News Directors Association
1717 K Street NW, Suite 615
Washington, DC 20006

Society of Professional Audio Recording Studios
4300 Tenth Avenue North, No. 2
Lake Worth, FL 33461

Touring Entertainment Industry Association (TEIA)
1203 Lake Street
Fort Worth, TX 76102

Women in Music
P.O. Box 441
Radio City Station
New York, NY 10101

For information on purchasing directories about colleges and universities that teach dance, including details on the types of courses offered and scholarships, write to:

National Dance Association
1900 Association Drive
Reston, VA 22091

A directory of dance, art and design, music, and theater programs may be purchased from:

National Association of Schools of Dance
11250 Roger Bacon Drive, Suite 21
Reston, VA 22090

For information on all aspects of dance, including job listings, send a self-addressed stamped envelope to:

American Dance Guild
31 West Twenty-first Street, Third Floor
New York, NY 10010

A directory of dance companies and related organizations, plus other information on professional dance, is available from:

Dance/USA
777 Fourteenth Street NW, Suite 540
Washington, DC 20005

About the Author

J an Goldberg's love for the printed page began well before her second birthday. Regular visits to the book bindery where her grandfather worked produced a magic combination of sights and smells that she carries with her to this day.

Childhood was filled with composing poems and stories, reading books, and playing library. Elementary and high school included an assortment of contributions to school newspapers. While a full-time college student, Goldberg wrote extensively as part of her job responsibilities in the College of Business Administration at Roosevelt University in Chicago. After receiving a degree in elementary education, she was able to extend her love of reading and writing to her students.

Goldberg has written extensively in the occupations area for General Learning Corporation's *Career World Magazine*, as well as for the many career publications produced by CASS Communications. She has also contributed to a number of projects for educational publishers, including Scott Foresman, Addison-Wesley, and Camp Fire Boys and Girls.

As a feature writer, Goldberg's work has appeared in *Parenting Magazine*, *Today's Chicago Woman*, *Opportunity Magazine*, *Chicago Parent*, *Correspondent*, *Opportunity Magazine*, *Successful Student*, *Complete Woman*, *North Shore Magazine*, and the Pioneer Press newspapers. In all, she has published more than 250 pieces as a freelance writer.

In addition to *Careers for Color Connoisseurs*, she is the author of more than a dozen career books published by NTC/Contemporary Publishing Group. She also recently completed four Capstone High/Low Books for elementary school students: *Private Investigator*, *Fire Fighter*, *Medical Record Technician*, and *Security Guard*.